Lecture Notes in Artificial Intelligence

Subseries of Lecture Notes in Computer Science
Edited by J. Siekmann

Lecture Notes in Computer Science

Edited by G. Goos and J. Hartmanis

J. Hertzberg (Ed.)

European Workshop on Planning

EWSP '91, Sankt Augustin, FRG
March 18-19, 1991
Proceedings

Springer-Verlag

Berlin Heidelberg New York
London Paris Tokyo
Hong Kong Barcelona
Budapest

Series Editor

Jörg Siekmann
Institut für Informatik, Universität Kaiserslautern
Postfach 3049, W-6750 Kaiserslautern, FRG

Volume Editor

Joachim Hertzberg
Gesellschaft für Mathematik und Datenverarbeitung, GMD
Schloß Birlinghoven, W-5205 Sankt Augustin, FRG

CR Subject Classification (1991): I.2.8, J.1

ISBN 3-540-54364-3 Springer-Verlag Berlin Heidelberg New York
ISBN 0-387-54364-3 Springer-Verlag New York Berlin Heidelberg

© Springer-Verlag Berlin Heidelberg 1991
Printed in Germany

Typesetting: Camera ready by author
Printing and binding: Druckhaus Beltz, Hemsbach/Bergstr.
2145/3140-543210 - Printed on acid-free paper

Preface

Planning – formulating a course of action – and related fields like scheduling or reasoning about action have a long research tradition in AI with many researchers all over the world working in them. Judging from text sources like the *Readings in Planning**, it seems obvious that most of the planning research is done in the United States, but there has always been such research in Europe, too.

However, it seems that there is a communication problem among us European planning researchers: many of us are not well aware of the good work done nextdoor. There are a few national interest groups for planning (e.g., in the UK and in the FRG), resulting, to some degree, in national scenes; however, for most of us this situation is far from providing the stimulating atmosphere that seems possible when bringing together many people with different backgrounds and different experiences but with a common interest in planning.

The European Workshop on Planning (EWSP) was an attempt to provide such an atmosphere. It took place March 18–19, 1991, in GMD's Schloss Birlinghoven at Sankt Augustin near Bonn, with about 60 participants. The papers presented were selected by a programme committee; 10 of the 27 submitted papers are included in this proceedings volume.

There were actually a few more talks during the workshop than reflected by these 10 papers. The reason for that, I think, is part of our communication problem: the refereeing process showed widely different assessments of the contributions of individual papers. It is normal that referees disagree; however, the frequency and the grade of disagreement here were such that the committee decided to have a number of papers presented and discussed on which the referees disagreed considerably but which were judged to deal with interesting topics anyway. (This volume contains only papers rejected by none of their referees.)

Such differences in opinion were the more surprising as there seems to be a trend in the European planning research towards formalization of planning and action, which refutes the seemingly obvious assumption that the differences are yet another instance of a theoreticians versus practitioners squabble. There must be other reasons, and one of these might be the very lack of coherence of the European planning community.

There is a certain stress on formal planning work mirrored in the papers in this volume, which has its counterpart in a certain shortness of application work. Moreover, there are important and interesting areas related to planning that are totally missing here, e.g., plan recognition or cognitive aspects of planning. The papers submitted for and those presented at the EWSP, of which the papers in this volume are a good profile, are certainly not representative for the field of planning as a whole. But couldn't this very concentration be the germ of coherence of a *European* planning scene?

---

* Allen, J., Hendler, J., Tate, A. (eds.): Readings in Planning. San Mateo: Morgan Kaufmann, 1990

I would like to thank all people who have submitted papers, independently of whether they have been accepted or not. A workshop, first of all, lives by the authors taking the time to write their ideas down and to submit. Second, a workshop lives by the programme committee and all those taking the time to referee; thanks to all the people listed below. Third, a workshop lives by support, be it moral or cash. ECCAI, GI, and GMD have supported the EWSP in one way or another; thanks to all of them. Fourth, a workshop lives by organizing lots of tiny details; thanks to all the GMD colleagues who have helped me with that. And fifth, a workshop – most importantly – lives by its participants leading lively discussions; we had these, for the benefit of us all.

Sankt Augustin, April 1991   Joachim Hertzberg

Programme Committee

Wolfgang Bibel, TH Darmstadt, FRG

Joachim Hertzberg, GMD, Sankt Augustin, FRG (chair)

Hermann Kaindl, Siemens AG, Wien, Austria

Albrecht Kellner, MBB Erno, Bremen, FRG

Erik Sandewall, Linköping Univ., Sweden

Nigel Shadbolt, Nottingham Univ., UK

Austin Tate, AIAI, Edinburgh, UK

List of Reviewers

Ken Currie

Brian Drabble

Uwe Egly

Bertram Fronhöfer

Tom Gordon

Gerd Große

Steffen Hölldobler

Alexander Horz

Frank v. Martial

Siegfried Meggendorfer

Han Reichgelt

Josef Schneeberger

Contents

HELP - A Hierarchical Execution-Led Planner for Robotic Domains

Ruth Aylett,

National Advanced Robotics Centre,

University Rd., Salford, M5 4PP, UK.

email: R.Aylett@uk.ac.salford.sysc

Alan Fish,

SD-Scicon,

Abney Hall, Manchester Rd., Cheadle, Cheshire, UK

Simon Bartrum,

SD-Scicon,

Abney Hall, Manchester Rd., Cheadle, Cheshire, UK

Abstract:

HELP has been developed as a prototype of part of the functionality of a generic robot architecture. We discuss its main features and highlight execution-led planning and planning 'moods' as two ways of coming to terms with the planner's lack of complete and accurate knowledge of the real world.

Introduction.

Many planners have been built in robotic domains (e.g. STRIPS - Fikes and Nilsson 1971, FORBIN - Miller, Firby and Dean 1985, SIPE - Wilkins 1988, SPAR - Hutchinson and Kak 1990) and it is common knowledge that such domains pose particular problems for task planners. The assumption made by some classical systems that the planner has access to complete and accurate knowledge of the world (Hendler, Tate, Drummond 1990) is untenable in such domains for a number of reasons. Firstly, the logical world model is derived from the input of sensors which may provide inaccurate, incomplete or ambiguous information. Secondly, the world is not normally wholly accessible to the sensors at any one time (sensory limitation). Thirdly, the world may be changed by agents and processes within it which are independent of the robot. Fourthly, the robot is a real rather than an ideal mechanism and may not behave quite as the planner assumes.

These problems have influenced the design of HELP, which has been developed not for a particular robotic domain but as a prototype[1] for some of the functionality of a generic architecture for semi-autonomous robots - both mobiles and manipulators. We will briefly discuss the general view of task planning taken within this architecture.

Task planning in the Generic Architecture

The generic architecture embodies three levels of functionality - the executive, the tactical and the strategic. Executive functions are conventionally engineered using real-time techniques giving a cycle time of 1m sec or less. These systems are algorithmic and perform synchronously, including such functions as trajectory tracking, sensor tracking and reactive safety.

Tactical functions are also largely synchronous and algorithmic, with cycle times of 20m secs or less. Here we have functions such as data integration, feature tracking, trajectory planning and monitoring. The strategic level, in contrast, is intended to work asynchronously with

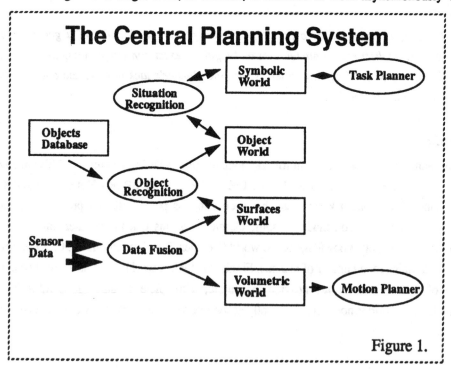

Figure 1.

---

1. HELP is implemented in Prolog within the Poplog environment.

much longer cycle times, possibly up to a few minutes. Here we have AI systems such as the task planner along with other planning agents; also world models and model-building agents.

The three levels of functionality are embodied in three large-scale modules within the architecture: input, output and central planning. The input and output modules largely function at the executive and tactical levels - it is the central planning system (CPS) module which incorporates most of the strategic level of the system. Fig. 1 shows the CPS organised round a hierarchy of world models, with a very primitive volumetric world model at the lowest level, and the symbolic world - which supports the task planner - at the highest level.

The symbolic world is therefore many levels removed from sensor data, underlining the point made above about its incompleteness and inaccuracy. In contrast, the motion planner - which constructs collision-free paths under the direction of the task planner - works on a very primitive world model which is close to the sensors and is likely to be far more accurate and complete. The trade-off is its lack of knowledge - it maps free and occupied space only, and has no conception of objects.

The HELP prototype

In Fig. 2 we see the overall architecture of the HELP system. In it are implemented both the task planning function of the generic architecture and the symbolic world modelling function, while it also contains an executive embodying an embryonic form of a control structure for the generic architecture. It does not contain the object world or other world models from Fig.

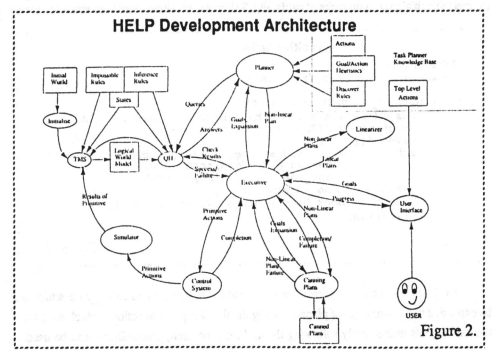

Figure 2.

1, nor any of the processes that work on those worlds such as motion planning. Neither does it concern itself with functions which fall into the tactical layer of the architecture, notably collision-avoidance, which from the level of the task planner can be seen as a reflex.

Clearly a final version of the task planner will require interfaces with other components: for instance it must be able to communicate at the level of its primitive move actions with the motion planner, which in turn will report the success or failure of the primitive's execution. In the same way, it must also be able to communicate indirectly with input sensors where its primitives are concerned with finding out information. However in HELP these interfaces are hidden within the simulator.

We will now go on to discuss the most important components of the architecture shown in Fig. 2.

The Task Planner and Planner Knowledge Base

HELP contains a hierarchical non-linear planner modelled on systems such as NOAH (Sacerdoti 1977) and NONLIN (Tate 1975). The planner must be configured for a specific domain by designing a planner knowledge base for it containing the hierarchy of actions, goal and action heuristics, 'discover rules' for finding out unknown information, and top-level actions through which the user may interact with the planner. We will give an example of each of these from a (somewhat idealised) satellite maintenance domain in which a robot, with a selection of special-purpose hands, maintains Orbital Replacement Units (ORUs) stored in cabinets which also contain racks of cards. Fig. 3 shows a primitive - that is executable - action

```
                    A Primitive Action
/* DETACH HAND */
/* Remove current hand from arm */

action (detach_hand (Hand, Point),
        text ('Detach @ from the arm to @', [Hand, Point]),
        constraints ([Hand \= none]),
        given ([]),
        achieve ([dock_hand_storage (Point, vacant):consumed,
                  hand_on_arm (Hand):consumed,
                  hand_position (Point):used]),
        results ([hand_on_arm (none),
                  dock_hand_storage (Point, Hand)]),
        primitive).
```

Figure 3.

detach_hand, while Fig. 4 illustrates a hierarchical action deinstall_oru which can be expanded to a lower level of planning using the listed expansion actions, which are passed the list of goals immediately following them. As can be seen, preconditions can be used or

---

An Expandable Action

```
/* DEINSTALL ORU */
/* Deinstall an ORU when on the docking pad */

action (deinstall_oru (ORU, Oru_slot, Unit, Dock),
        text ('Deinstall @ from @ at @',
              [ORU, Oru_slot, Unit]),
        constraints ([qh (oru (ORU))]),
        given ([]),
        achieve ([oru_slot_state (Oru_slot, ORU):consumed,
                  oru_slot_in_unit(Oru_slot, Unit):used,
                  unit_at_dock (Unit, Dock):used,
                  robots_docking_position (Dock):used]),
        results ([holding (ORU),
                  oru_slot_state (Oru_slot, vacant)]),
        expansion ([select_hand,
                    hold_item,
                    pull_out_oru,
                    wait_for_oru],
                   [oru_slot_state (Oru_slot, vacant)]).
```

Figure 4.

---

consumed in the usual way, variables in the action can have their value constrained once instantiated, while 'givens' can instantiate variables as soon as the action is selected.

Both actions and goals can be ordered by heuristics, which may be domain specific or domain independent. So for example, an action heuristic might order actions according to their number of preconditions, or it might specify that if both deinstall_oru and open_cover are available, the latter should be tried first. Likewise a goal heuristic might order goals according to the number of variables in each, or it might force the goal rack_slot_state to be satisfied before others.

'Discover' rules may be used by the planner to find out unknown information - though it has to be in the right 'mood' to do this as we will see later. So if the contents of a rack slot are not known by the robot, a rule to pull out the rack will allow it to find this out, or if it is not known whether a board is faulty or not, a rule to examine its status can be provided. Finally top-level actions package the achievable goals for presentation to the user, prompting for required values in the selected goal.

Execution-Led Planning.

Most classical planners - STRIPS (Fikes and Nilsson 1971), NOAH (Sacerdoti 1977), NONLIN (Tate 1975), SIPE (Wilkins 1988) for example - constructed a whole plan before attempting to execute it, with execution monitoring to detect plan fails and a replanning capacity to patch a failing plan. The advantage of this approach is that the problems of planning can be considered on their own - in particular those concerning the correctness and efficiency of plans. However it depends heavily on the assumption that the planner has a complete and accurate world model, which as already noted is quite unrealistic in robotic domains.

An alternative is to interleave planning and execution in some way, as McDermott suggested in his work round NASL (McDermott 1978). He saw this as closer to the human approach to problem-solving - itself determined by the need to work with wrong and incomplete information - which he characterised as 'try something, wait until an error has been made, and then correct it.' Thus NASL picked a task, executed it if it was a primitive, and otherwise reduced it. However it depended on an explicit description of the subtask network rather than on generalised non-linear planning, with special choice rules to ensure that only one reduction could be made.

If time is an explicit part of the planning model, interleaving planning and execution at the strategic level through task-scheduling become issues, as in FORBIN (Miller, Firby, Dean 1985). FORBIN however, was developed for a domain (the robot warehouse worker) in which the future was at least stochastically predictable and the environment relatively benevolent, an assumption that cannot be made in general for robotic domains. The mechanism adopted in HELP therefore is closer to that of PRS (Georgeff and Lansky 1987), but unlike PRS is combined with the classical technique of hierarchical non-linear planning.

Initially the executive calls the planner within HELP to produce a skeleton plan using root actions only, without expanding any of the hierarchical definitions. So in the satellite domain, a high-level non-linear plan would be built using the 'root' actions `fix_unit`, `fetch_item`, `store_item`, `deinstall_board`, `release_item`, `install_board`, `deinstall_board`, and `install_oru`. The executive then passes the plan to the linearizer which passes back a linear version for presentation to the user. If the plan is approved, the first action will be executed if it is a primitive, otherwise the planner will be reinvoked to expand it into a new non-linear plan. Thus if the first action in the high-level plan had been `deinstall_oru`, the planner would expand it into a new non-linear plan using `select_hand`, `hold_item`, `pull_out_oru`, `wait_for_oru` which has as its goal `oru_slot_state (Oru_slot, vacant)`. As soon as a primitive action is encountered, it is executed, so that the way in which planning and execution will be interleaved depends substantially on the design of the action hierarchy.

There are a number of advantages to this approach in the type of domain targeted. Firstly, if the preconditions of an action fail on execution, or if the expected results fail to occur, the planner is simply reinvoked from the current level, with its initial state now including all actions executed up to that point. Even if the worst comes to the worst, and the whole of the initial high-level plan has to be thrown away, most of it will be unexpanded, so that relatively little effort is wasted. Secondly, fails that result from the unreliability of the world model are reduced by the postponement of detailed planning. In particular, fails due to sensory limitation should be reduced: for instance the robot is likely to have already executed the part of the plan which takes it round the corner before it expands the part of the plan which wants to know if the door is locked. As Georgeff and Lansky comment: "In many domains, information how best to achieve a given goal is acquired during plan execution." (Georgeff and Lansky, 1987). Finally the computational costs of planning and replanning are spread over the execution period and may be implemented in parallel with those required for execution. In a real-time environment this is a serious consideration.

Since planning proceeds essentially depth-first, left-to-right, one might assume that the planner would be immune to the problem of 'hierarchical promiscuity' described by Wilkins (Wilkins 1988) in his critique of classical task planning. This problem arises when the action hierarchy is really a graph, that is to say a given primitive (or other action) appears in the expansion of more than one action. In this case the preconditions of an action at a higher but further right branch of a given plan tree may be invalidated by the effects of an action lower but more to the left in the tree, since higher-level actions will be incorporated into a plan at that level of abstraction first.

Unfortunately, since a whole plan is constructed at a given level of abstraction before the depth-first expansion is pursued, it *is* possible for this situation to arise within HELP. To combat it, it is necessary for significant effects of actions in an expansion to be attached to the parent action, taking into account the preconditions of all other actions available at that level of abstraction. Though this places a burden on the implementor within a particular domain, it is not felt to be an unreasonably heavy one.

The approach has other disadvantages of course. Because the plan is generated incrementally, it may be less efficient than one wholly expanded at 'plan time'. It is also possible that if the user sets infeasible goals, HELP will not discover this until part-way through execution. Estimating the costs of achieving the given goals may not be straightforward and have to rely on heuristics. However the problems associated with generating complex and computationally expensive plans which then require major surgery on the fly are felt to be much greater in robotic domains.

World Modelling In HELP.

In the generic architecture, world modelling agents are separated from planning agents, and just as there is more than one planning agent there are also multiple world modelling agents - for example for the 'free-space' world used by the motion planner or the geometrical surfaces world resulting from data-fusion of sensor input. However the task planner is only concerned with the symbolic world model, so it is this alone that appears within HELP. The world model is accessed via a query-handler (qh) and a truth-maintenance system (tms) which not only manipulate explicit facts about the world but also make use of mechanisms for inferring others: inference rules, state information, and 'impossible' rules.These allow causal modelling within the world and thus provide a facility for coping with the consequences of the frame problem.In particular, the ability to infer side effects of actions relieves an implementor of the need to specify all possible consequences of an action within the action definition as was necessary in STRIPS.

So for example, in the satellite maintenance domain, an inference rule allows the query-handler to infer that if both securing pins on a rack slot are out, then the board slot is unlocked. The state information about objects in the domain also allows inferencing: board slots may only be one of the states 'unlocked' and 'locked', so that both tms and qh can infer from the truth of one the falsity of the other. Finally 'impossible' rules are used by tms to maintain consistency in the world when new facts are added: for instance if the robot installs a particular hand onto its arm, that hand can no longer be in its storage slot.

'Moods' as a response to the unknown.

While execution-led planning allows HELP to ignore the uncertainty of its world model to some extent, it doesn't provide a mechanism for dealing with statements which are *unknown* in the world model. Few planners have such a mechanism: SIPE (Wilkins 1988) for instance will fail if the truth values of critical predicates are not known. (Though it does provide the somewhat ad hoc mechanism of allowing the argument of a predicate of unknown truth value to be replaced by the symbol 'unknown').

One possible approach is to anticipate failure for plans involving the unknown and to incorporate extra plan actions for likely failures - take the key in case the door is locked - or to incorporate extra execution monitoring associated with fixes for failed tests - use sensors to determine state of door at execution time and if locked go get key (Hutchinson and Kak 1990, Kaelbling 1987). This gives a planner a cautious and conservative style which may well be appropriate in some domains, but not in others. An extreme version of this position is Schoppers' 'universal plans' (Schoppers 1987) in which plans contain conditional tests to deal with all possible execution-time contingencies. The costs of this solution appear too high for it to be applied in a domain-independent planner.

In designing HELP a number of different approaches to this issue were considered.The first was to avoid the problem altogether by ensuring that the query-handler would be able to answer any query from the planner. This would mean that when HELP was configured to a new domain, it would be necessary to produce a complete set of the inference rules referred to above together with a complete enumeration of all states applicable to objects in the world. Armed with complete information the query handler would always be able to establish the truth value of a query from the planner. We have already dismissed this option as utopian in robot domains.

A second option would be to have the query-handler assume that unknowns are false as just suggested - essentially the 'closed world' assumption. We have already argued that the resulting conservatism may not be justifiable in all domains.

A third option would be to allow the query-handler to assign default values to particular queries. Thus if board1 is not known to be functional or faulty, a default of functional could be specified on the basis that boards do not fail very often. This however is open to the same sort of objection as the first option: it requires the specification of a *complete* set of sensible defaults if it is to succeed. It seems unlikely that these could always be provided.

The option adopted resulted from analysis of the range of possible responses to the unknown, and the implications of each response in robot domains. One has already been discussed: the truth value of an unknown could be assumed false. However, equally, the truth value could be assumed true. Two other responses are also possible: the planner could abandon any line of reasoning depending on queries returning 'unknown', and the planner could plan to find out the truth value of the unknown statement through extra sensor actions as already mentioned. Each of these planning attitudes or 'moods' could be valuable in particular domains.

For instance, assuming false for unknowns - the *pessimist* approach - would lead the planner to fail the current goal and seek to resatisfy it. As already argued, this would produce conservative planning behaviour and result in a robot spending time and resources preparing for the worst case. Assume a goal is to have a board functional and its state is unknown: it will be assumed faulty and the planner will seek actions resulting in it being functional. Thus a *pessimist* planning mood will limit plan failure at execution time together with the need for replanning, which could be very important in domains where this would be expensive. Imagine for example a robot on a mission - space or deep-sea. Here making a wrong assumption and 'going back' could be extremely costly.

In other domains assuming true for unknowns - the *optimist* stance - could be a sensible approach. Here if a door was required to be open during planning and its state was unknown, the planner would assume it was indeed open. This describes a world which is set up for the robot's convenience - such as the FORBIN warehouse. In this type of environment humans are in control and ensure that everything is left as required by the robot.

The third approach, of abandoning reasoning involving unknowns could be described as *fatalist*. It might be appropriate in domains where a robot could not afford to make any incorrect assumption, true or false, and is unlikely to have time to find out the correct values, but must plan with definite facts known to be true or false. Note that in this mood there is a higher probability of the planner ending up with no plan at all.

Finally, the stance of finding the value of unknowns - the *scientist* approach - might be sensible in environments where certainty is important but the costs in time and resources of finding out are not critical. Safety-critical environments such as a nuclear power station or a satellite or space-station might be appropriate for such behaviour. It is in this 'mood' that the planner can make use of the 'discover' rules mentioned above.

The global nature of the planning attitudes just discussed makes it inadvisable to hardwire one or other of them into HELP. Better to see them as a repertoire available both to the planner and to the user of the system, whether at configuration to a new domain or indeed using the system within a domain. Planning moods are therefore user selectable before planning begins.

Planner directed mood change.

Given the different characteristics of the planning moods, it seemed advantageous to allow the planner to change attitude 'in flight' as well as allowing the user to set an initial mood. As a first step, upper and lower thresholds were defined, with the former linked to high planning cost, and the latter to low planning success.

Planning cost was measured by the rate at which links were added and removed during planning, with a user-set upper threshold such that if cost rose above the threshold a change in mood would be triggered. This change would depend on the existing mood: if *scientist*, then change to *pessimist*, if *pessimist* then change to *fatalist*, if *fatalist* then change to *optimist*. This chain of moods orders them according to the amount of extra planning effort they are expected to generate - if planning costs become 'too high' then planning effort is reduced.

Planning success was measured by monitoring the success and failure of actions depending upon mood-determined assumptions. Again the user is allowed to set a threshold: in this case a change in mood is triggered by success falling below the threshold. The change again depends on the initial mood: from *optimist* to *fatalist*, from *fatalist* to *pessimist*, from *pessimist* to *scientist*. Here if the success rate is 'too low' a more cautious approach involving greater planning effort is made.

In practice this mechanism has not proved entirely successful: it is difficult to decide threshold levels other than ad hoc. Moreover, the success rate relies on actions with assumed information, which in practice are few, so that success rate is rarely updated. Two other mechanisms are currently under consideration, though neither has as yet been implemented.

The first of these is to allow the attachment of moods to goals. For example, consider a stock-control robot in a warehouse. The *optimist* attitude could be attached to the goal `path_state(Path,clear)` since we could assume that the robot's paths are usually kept clear. The *pessimist* attitude could be attached to the goal `shelf_state(Shelf,empty)` as shelves are rarely empty. The *scientist* attitude could be attached to the goal `items_on_shelf(Shelf,Items)` since what is on a particular shelf needs to be discovered, and cannot meaningfully be assumed true or false.

The advantages of this approach are that good control is maintained over how goals are handled within planning, while the goals referenced could be as general or specific as required. On the other hand, it may be difficult to decide which goals should be tagged and how, while it seems possible that the best tag to attach to a goal may depend on the planning context in which it appears. This approach would also make the planner's mood very changeable since goals with different moods attached might follow in rapid succession.

A more plausible alternative would be to tag actions rather than goals. Consider a fire-fighting robot involved in putting out fires and rescuing people. One might wish to tag the action `lift_object (injured_person)` with *pessimist* so that the planner will act conservatively without planning a full medical checkup to determine the actual extent of injuries. On the other hand, the action `fetch_object(fire_extinguisher)` could be tagged with the *scientist* mood so that its location could be discovered and its state (working/faulty, full/empty) could be determined. Now the planning mood will remain constant throughout a given level of planning since it will only change on the execution of an action. Moreover goals will still be indirectly referenced via the arguments to actions: the action `fetch_object(fire_extinguisher)` contains the specified argument in the goal `holding(fire_extinguisher)`.

Conclusion.

We have discussed the features of the prototype world-modelling and task-planning systems embodied in the HELP system. Though based classic non-linear planning techniques, the incorporation of execution-led planning and planning 'moods' are intended to adapt it to the uncertainty of robotic domains.

Apart from further development of the mood mechanism as discussed above, it is intended to incorporate explanation of plan fails for the operator as well as changing from a purely logical to an object-oriented representation for the symbolic world. However the most substantial planned development is the conversion of the whole system into a 'live' version on parallel hardware linked in to the other components of the generic architecture.

References

Dean, T. L., 1987. Intractability and Time-Dependent Planning. *Reasoning about Actions and plans: Proceedings of the 1986 Workshop*, eds M. Georgeff and A. Lansky,. San Mateo, Calif.: Morgan Kaufmann.

Fikes, R. E. and Nilsson, N. J., 1971. Strips: A New Approach to the Application of Theorem-Proving to Problem-Solving. *Artificial Intelligence* 2: pp189-208

Georgeff, M. P. and Lansky, A. 1987. Reactive Reasoning and Planning. *Proceedings of the Sixth National Conference on Artificial Intelligence.* Menlo Park, Calif.: American Association for Artificial Intelligence.

Hendler, J.; Tate, A. and Drummond, M. 1990. AI Planning: Systems and Techniques. *AI Magazine*, Vol. 11, No. 2, Summer 1990, pp61-77.

Hutchinson, S. A. and Kak, A. C. 1990. Spar: A Planner That Satisfies Operational and Geometrical Constraints in Uncertain Environments. *AI Magazine*, Vol. 11, No. 1, Spring 1990, pp31-61.

Kaelbling, L. 1987. An Architecture for Intelligent Reactive Systems. *Reasoning about Actions and plans: Proceedings of the 1986 Workshop*, eds M. Georgeff and A. Lansky,. San Mateo, Calif.: Morgan Kaufmann.

McDermott, D. 1978. Planning and Acting. *Cognitive Science*, v 2, pp71-109

Miller, D.; Firby, J. and Dean, T. 1985. Deadlines, Travel Time, and Robot Problem Solving. *Proceedings of the Ninth International Joint Conference on Artificial Intelligence.* Menlo Park, Calif.: International Joint Conferences on Artificial Intelligence.

Sacerdoti, E. D., 1977. *A Structure for Plans and Behaviour.* Amsterdam: Elsevier-North Holland

Schoppers, M. 1987. Universal plans for Reactive Robots in Unpredictable Domains. In *Proceedings of the Tenth International Joint Conference on Artificial Intelligence.* Menlo Park, Calif.: International Joint Conferences on Artificial Intelligence.

Tate, A. 1975. Project Planning Using a Hierarchical Non-Linear Planner. Report 25, Dept. Artificial Intelligence, Edinburgh.

Wilkins, D.E. 1988. *Practical Planning - Extending the Classical AI Planning Paradigm.* San Mateo, Calif.: Morgan Kaufmann.

Integrating classical and reactive planning within an architecture for autonomous agents

Joseph Downs and Han Reichgelt*
AI Group
Department of Psychology
University of Nottingham
Nottingham NG7 2RD
England
jd@psyc.nott.ac.uk, han@psyc.nott.ac.uk

Abstract

In this paper we describe an architecture for agents that have to act in dynamic environments. The architecture, which has been partially implemented in Common Lisp, consists of a number of layers, each of which occupies a different position on the flexibility versus computational tractability trade-off. By integrating a high-level declarative planner with a reactive planner using situated-action rules, the architecture combines the flexibility of the former with the efficiency of the latter. Moreover, the lower levels of the architecture can be automatically configured on the basis of previous activities of the higher levels, thus avoiding the need for providing a complete set of situated-action rules that is inherent in a purely reactive planning approach.

1 Introduction

The predominant view of goal-directed agent activity in AI is based upon the 'Plan, then Execute' strategy (Ambros-Ingerson, 1986). In this model a plan of action must be synthesised in its entirety before a separate execution phase can begin in which the agent attempts to carry out the actions specified by the plan. This latter phase requires plan monitoring which checks that actions achieve their expected results and that the environment has not changed in such a way as to render successful execution of the plan impossible. Should plan execution fail (because a necessary action never achieves its postconditions or because

---

*We would like to thank George Kiss and Nigel Shadbolt for valuable discussions. We would also like to thank a number of anonymous referees who make useful comments on an earlier draft of this paper. The first author is financially supported by an SERC postgraduate studentship.

its preconditions never become true), then replanning is necessary. This usually involves discarding all or most of the original plan, thus wasting a lot of the earlier planning effort. In addition, the most powerful and general planners developed within this approach, i.e. hierarchical and non-linear, are subject to several combinatorial explosions (Chapman, 1987). These two problems result in the classical planning architecture being unsuitable for complex and/or dynamic domains. This is perhaps most clearly demonstrated by the fact that the archetypical planning domain is the blocks-world which contains relatively few objects and assumes that a single agent, controlling the robot-arm, is the only entity capable of changing the environment.

There have been attempts within the classical planning paradigm to overcome these limitations. Thus, both IPEM (Ambros-Ingerson and Steel, 1988) and SIPE (Wilkins, 1985) can interleave the processes of plan formation and execution. SIPE additionally offers faster plan generation (Wilkins, 1988). However, none of these seem to offer an entirely satisfactory solution to the problem. As a result, a more radical solution has recently been offered. This approach is known as 'reactive planning' or 'situated action', e.g. Rosenschein (1985), Agre and Chapman (1987), Firby (1987), Georgeff and Lansky (1987), Schoppers (1987), and Drummond (1989). The basis of this approach is that real-time performance from agents which are embedded in complex domains can be achieved by some form of direct mapping from situations (i.e. particular conditions holding in the environment) to actions. This situation-action mapping needs to give wide (or even complete) coverage of the possible situations that can occur in the environment and perform actions which usually (or even always) advance the agent towards achieving its (pre-specified) goals. This method has the advantage that with a sufficiently well-designed mapping the agent can react appropriately to sudden changes in the environment in a timely manner since, in the simplest examples of reactive planning, all that is required to initiate an action is to examine the sensors and use their readings to index a look-up table of responses without having to engage in any time-consuming search process.

This initial outline may seem to imply that reactive planning is essentially advocating behaviourism under a different name. While this may be the case for the most simplistic reactive systems, this charge cannot be laid against more sophisticated reactive planning systems. Systems of this kind allow for internal states, representing such things as goals, beliefs, values etc. Actions are then selected on the basis of internal state in conjunction with the external world state. Such systems therefore need not always select the same action in the same world state and their behaviour is not fully contingent upon the environment. Furthermore, the situation-action mapping may take its inputs from the outputs of a perception module rather than using 'raw' sensor readings, thus providing higher-level (and more useful) situation descriptions for the agent to base its action decisions upon than is available from unprocessed sensor readings.

It should be noted however that there is some disagreement amongst researchers of reactive planning as to the status of such planners with respect to classical planning, based upon the question of how expressive the agent's internal representations should be. Agre and Chapman's work (Agre 1988; Agre and Chapman 1987, 1988; Chapman and Agre 1986) espouses an interactionist philosophy, claiming that much structured behaviour arises naturally from the agent reflecting the structure of the world in which it is embedded. This leads them to the claim that deictic representations of minimal complexity, called 'indexical-functionals', are sufficient to mediate much routine, seemingly plan-following, activity. The classical planning paradigm is thus rejected as being of little or no use in the construction of agents intended to operate outside logic-puzzle style blocks-world domains.

Most other researchers are more sympathetic to the classical planning paradigm. They draw attention to the fact that reactive planners are 'myopic' in the sense that they can only satisfactorily react in situations for which they have a matching situation-action rule. Designers of reactive planners therefore have to think in advance of all possible situations the system may find itself in. However, this is impossible for all but the simplest types of task, and it is therefore very likely the agent will encounter a situation in the world for which its reaction plan provides no response (or at least no useful response). In such unanticipated situations the agent might need to invoke a classical planner to decide what to do. Clearly, it would be advantageous if the result of these calls to a classical planner could be compiled into further situation-action rules which could then be used if the agent were to find itself in a similar situation again (Cf Russell, 1989). Under this view, reactive plans can be seen as an efficient run-time method for the results of previous high-level problem solving activities (such as classical planning). Our own research falls within this school of thought.

In this paper, we describe a preliminary implementation based on these ideas. Section 2 of this paper outlines the general framework of our proposed agent architecture. Section 3 details TEST, its planning component, and section 4 describes SITACT, an incremental compiler for TEST plans which returns relatively high-level situation-action rules intended for further decomposition into a language that can be used to direct robots. The current implementation does not, as yet, decompose the actions proposed by SITACT into a robot language. We return to this limitation in section 5. Section 6 concludes.

2 The Overall Agent Architecture

Figure 1 shows the components of our proposed agent architecture. This architecture is intended for use in domains which are neither entirely static, such as the traditional formulation of the blocks-world, nor entirely dynamic, such as video games. In the former type of domain, classical planners (such as NONLIN) are sufficient while in the latter only 'pure' reactive planners (such as Agre and Chapman's Pengi) are useful. Instead our architecture is intended for domains which have some dynamic elements but in which the 'pace of life' is not so frantic that the agent never has sufficient time to engage in classical planning.

In many AI applications, there is a fundamental trade-off between representational power and computational tractability (Levesque and Brachman, 1985). Planning is no exception. The different layers in our architecture occupy different positions on this trade-off. Thus,

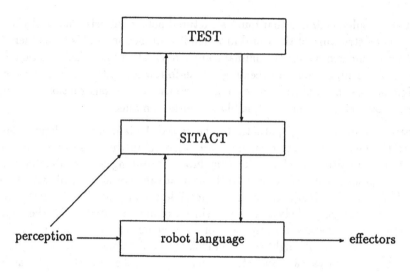

Figure 1: The agent architecture

as one moves up through the different levels, flexibility increases but computational efficiency decreases. TEST is a very high-level specification system for planners. SITACT is an interpreter for situation-action rules, which are automatically derived from TEST-generated plans. Finally, the lowest level is the level at which the system interacts with the world, either through sensors or via effectors. The architecture assumes that it is possible to translate the kind of primitives used in robot languages into higher-level primitives. In this paper, we will concentrate on TEST (section 3) and SITACT (section 4). We will briefly return to the lowest level in our architecture in section 5.

A fruitful analogy for the description of our architecture can be drawn with the relationship between high-level programming languages and assembly code. The lowest level provides the assembly language into which the high-level language of TEST has to be translated. This is achieved by using SITACT as a compiler which provides an intermediate level of description.

3 TEST

TEST (Reichgelt and Shadbolt, 1989, 1990) is a tool for specifying planning systems, implemented in Common Lisp. It is based on the assumption that logic has many advantages as a knowledge representation language. However, there are a number of applications where the purely deductive style of reasoning of logic is not sufficient. One example is default reasoning (Reichgelt, 1988). Following Israel (1980), Reichgelt argues that defaults should be seen as policies for belief fixation and revision. He therefore analyses them as instructions to the reasoning systems to make further assumptions about the world as and when the need arises. The process of adding assumptions about the world to the system's knowledge base is called "theory extension".

Reichgelt and Shadbolt argue that a purely deductive view of planning is not possible either, at least not if we move beyond the STRIPS assumptions underlying the situation calculus. Using Allen's reified logic of action and time (Allen, 1984), they argue that a plan can be seen as a set of statements saying that certain actions will occur at certain intervals in time. The question then arises how to formulate the relationship between the preconditions of an action and the occurrence of the action. A first possibility would be:

$$(true(free(hand), int(v, t)) \& true(clear(x), int(v', t))) \rightarrow$$
$$occurs(pick\text{-}up(x), int(t, t'))$$

where $int(t, t')$ indicates the interval starting at point t and ending at point t', $true$ indicates that the proposition is true over the interval, and $occurs$ that the action occurs over the interval. Unfortunately, this analysis is too strong. The fact that the preconditions of an action are true does not entail that the action must occur. In fact, all one can conclude from the truth of the preconditions is that the action is possible. This, however, suggests another formalization, namely, if the preconditions hold, then the action is possible:

$$(true(free(hand), int(v, t)) \& true(clear(x), int(v', t))) \rightarrow$$
$$\Diamond occurs(pick\text{-}up(x), int(t, t'))$$

But this analysis is too weak. All we can conclude from this operator description is that an action is possible. But a plan is a set of statements saying that particular actions *definitely* occur at certain intervals.

It is on the basis of these arguments that Reichgelt and Shadbolt argue that planning should also be seen as a form of theory extension. Propositions to the effect that some action occurs over some interval should then be regarded as possible assumptions that could in principle be added to the knowledge base, but only if the preconditions associated with the action are satisfied. Thus, $occurs(pick\text{-}up(x), int(t, t'))$ is regarded as an assumption that can be added to the knowledge base if $true(free(hand), int(v, t))$ and $true(clear(x), int(v', t))$ can be shown to hold. When the system is passed a goal, it will in general have to add a number of assumptions of the form $occurs(\phi, int(t, t'))$ to the knowledge base. The aim is to add enough assumptions to make the goal deductively derivable from the extended knowledge base. The plan can then be re-constructed from the set of assumptions added to the knowledge base.

The analysis of planning as theory extension has a number of consequences for the architecture of a problem solver. One still needs a knowledge base to store information about the world, and an inference engine to draw deductive inferences from this knowledge base. However, in addition, one needs an assumption pool in which those assumptions that the system can potentially add to its knowledge base are stored together with their associated preconditions, as well as an assumption manager, a component responsible for actually adding assumptions. TEST reflects this architecture.

An additional requirement is that the heuristics used by the inference engine and the assumption manager should be explicitly available for inspection and alteration. This flexibility facilitates the development and maintenance of systems. In TEST the user can change the heuristics used by the assumption manager. Thus, the user can change for example the way in which the preconditions associated with a potential assumption are proved, or the way in which assumptions are ordered if more than one is potentially relevant. This feature has allowed us to configure TEST not only for different planning applications but also for default applications. The drawback of this flexibility is relatively slow problem-solving.

The overall control regime used by TEST is as follows. The user passes a goal to TEST. It will initially try to derive this goal using deduction alone from the knowledge base. During the search for this proof, the theorem prover may reach a dead-end because some proposition cannot be derived from the knowledge base. It then calls the assumption manager in the hope that the proposition in question can in principle be added as an assumption. If this succeeds, the current proof continues; if it fails, the system backtracks.

The following is a very simple example. Suppose that we have the following initial situation:

$true(free(hand), int(t0, t1))$

$true(clear(a), int(t0, t1))$

$true(clear(b), int(t0, t1))$

We also have the following axioms describing the effects of different actions, which we call "operator descriptions"[1]:

$occurs(pick\text{-}up(x), int(t, t')) \rightarrow (\exists s)(true(held(x), int(t', s)) \& \neg true(free(hand), int(t', s)))$

$occurs(stack(x, y), int(t, t')) \rightarrow$
$\quad (\exists s)(true(on(x, y), int(t', s)) \& true(free(hand), int(t', s)) \& true(clear(x), int(t', s))$
$\quad\quad \& \neg true(clear(y), int(t', s)) \& \neg true(held(x), int(t', s)))$

Moreover, we have the following assumptions, together with their associated preconditions:

$occurs(pick\text{-}up(x), int(t, t'))$
preconditions: $(\exists s)(true(clear(x), int(s, t)) \& true(free(hand), int(s, t)))$

---

[1]Because of the way in which the current implementation derives situated action rules from TEST-generated plans, operator descriptions must contain all consequences of an action. An alternative formulation would associate a single "essential" consequence with each action and then contain a number of domain axioms which would describe the relationship between the "essential" consequence and other consequences. For example, our first operator description could be replaced by the following simpler operator description $occurs(pick\text{-}up(x), int(t, t')) \rightarrow (\exists s)(true(held(x), int(t', s)))$ plus the additional domain axiom $true(held(x), int(t, t')) \rightarrow \neg true(free(hand), int(t, t'))$ We return to this point in section 4.

$occurs(stack(x, y), int(t, t'))$
preconditions: $(\exists s)(true(clear(y), int(s, t))$ & $true(held(x), int(s, t)))$

nternally, axioms and entries in the assumption pool are skolemized before being stored. Thus, the two operator descriptions are internally stored as

$occurs(pick\text{-}up(x), int(t, t')) \rightarrow$
$\quad (true(held(x), int(t', sk1(x, t, t')))$ & $\neg true(free(hand), int(t', sk1(x, t, t'))))$

$occurs(stack(x, y), int(t, t')) \rightarrow$
$\quad (true(on(x, y), int(t', sk2(x, y, t, t')))$ & $true(free(hand), int(t', sk2(x, y, t, t')))$ &
$\quad\quad true(clear(x), int(t', sk2(x, y, t, t')))$ & $\neg true(clear(y), int(t', sk2(x, y, t, t')))$ &
$\quad\quad \neg true(held(x), int(t', sk2(x, y, t, t'))))$

where $sk1$ and $sk2$ are skolem functions.

TEST uses a semantic tableaux based theorem prover (see Elfrink and Reichgelt, 1989). The goal $(\exists t)(\exists t')(true(on(a, b), int(t, t')))$ is thus skolemized to $true(on(a, b), inter(t, t'))$. Using the second axiom, this can be reduced to $(occurs(stack(a, b), int(s, t)))^2$ with t' bound to $sk2(a, b, s, t)$. The theorem prover now reaches a dead-end and hands over to the assumption manager. The assumption manager retrieves the second assumption and tries to prove the precondition $(true(clear(b), int(s', s))$ & $true(held(a), int(s', s)))$. The second conjunct of this conjunction can be reduced to $occurs(pick\text{-}up(a), int(t'', s'))$, with s bound to $sk1(a, t'', s')$, which itself leads to the need for theory extension. Since the preconditions associated with the first assumption can be shown to be true immediately, the proposition $occurs(pick\text{-}up(a), int(t1, t2))$ is added to the knowledge base, where $t2$ is $sk1(a, t0, t1)$. This allows us to prove the preconditions associated with $occurs(stack(a, b), int(s, t))$ and the proposition $occurs(stack(a, b), int(t3, t4))$ is therefore added to the knowledge base, where $t3$ is a skolem function depending on a and $t2$, and $t4$ a skolem term depending on a, b and $t3$. We can now prove the original goal from the extended knowledge base. The plan is the assumptions that have been added: $occurs(pick\text{-}up(a), int(t1, t2))$ and $occurs(stack(a, b), int(t3, t4))$.

4 SITACT

TEST-generated plans are used as input by SITACT which will convert them into situation-action rules. These rules can later be used to control the agent's activities without the need to resort to planning unless an entirely novel situation is encountered.

---

[2]In the discussion of this example, we will largely ignore the problem of variable passing. Moreover, we will assume a solution to the frame problem. Given that the frame problem is an instance of default reasoning, and that we analyze default reasoning as involving theory extension, it will come as no surprise that our solution to the frame problem relies on the addition of a further assumption to the assumption pool. Further details can be found in Reichgelt and Shadbolt (1990).

A situation-action rule for a goal at the SITACT level simply consists of a list of predicates describing the world (the situation) which is associated with a predicate describing the action to be performed in that world state so as to progress the agent towards achieving its goal. Situation and action descriptions are identical to those used by TEST[3]. It is the intended task of the perception module to derive such high-level descriptions of the world and the task of the back-end of SITACT to decompose action descriptions to a granularity closer to the level of muscular movements which is appropriate for the underlying robot language.

The following are two possible situation-action rules for the goal $on(a, b)$. They were generated from the example discussed in section 3:

IF $clear(a), clear(b), free(hand)$
   THEN $pick\text{-}up(a)$

IF $clear(b), held(a)$
   THEN $stack(a, b)$

The situation-action rules are derived in the following way. The SITACT module receives from TEST a plan of actions in the form of a record of which assumptions were invoked to prove the goal. Each assumption consists of an action and the time interval over which it occurred. In order to derive situation-action rules from such plan the following set of steps occurs:

1. Actions in the plan are temporally ordered. This can be done using the temporal ordering of the intervals over which the actions are assumed to occur.

2. The description of the initial situation in the TEST specification is assigned as the 'immediate situation'. The first action in the ordering from step (1) is similarly designated the 'immediate action'.

3. The 'immediate situation' is associated with the 'immediate action'. This then forms one situation-action rule for the goal.

4. The 'immediate situation' is updated by simulating the effect of performing the 'immediate action' in the 'immediate situation', based on the simulation assumption of successful execution in a static environment. This simulation is achieved by the use of operator-effect templates which specify the changes to be made to particular predicates in a situation description. Such templates are STRIPS-like in the sense that they are equivalent to the use of add and delete lists for predicates in a situation description and that no changes other than those specified in the templates are assumed to occur. The templates can be derived automatically from the operator descriptions used by TEST. The add list consists of all the non-negated predicates

---

[3]Obviously, syntactically the situation and action descriptions are different. In SITACT, they are predicates. In TEST, which uses a reified language, they are functions.

in the consequent, the delete list of all negated predicates[4]. Thus, the first operator description in the previous section would lead to the following template:

pick-up(x)
    add: *held*(x)
    delete: *free*(*hand*)

5. We set the 'immediate action' to the next action in the plan if there is one, and we go to step (3). Otherwise, the procedure terminates.

It should be noted that the 'immediate situation' used in the above outline is not intended to be an up-to-date description of the actual world state at the time of rule derivation. It is simply a projected world state description updated at each cycle of the derivation process on the assumption of problem-free later execution. However, one could imagine interleaving rule derivation with the actual execution of planned actions (provided the world has remained static) to achieve improved agent performance.

In order to improve performance of the entire architecture, we provide two facilities to extend the knowledge of the agent prior to its actual embedding in the environment. First, the designer can 'hard-wire' the agent with situation-action rules which achieve goals in situations that it is anticipated will be frequently encountered by the agent when it is actually embedded in the world. Hence, the agent need not begin as a tabula rasa and be disadvantaged by initially having to spend all its time in plan generation. Second, the top two layers of the architecture can be used externally to the domain to allow for "off-line" planning. This is effected by simulating the intended execution domain within the SITACT module. The user first supplies a situation description and a goal. Then, if no situation-action rule exists for that goal in that situation, TEST is invoked to produce a plan to achieve the goal given the situation description as part of its initial world state, and subsequently new situation-action rules are derived from that plan. If a situation-action rule does exist, its execution can be simulated using the operator effect templates to generate a new situation description, and the process is repeated. Morever, at each cycle through this generate-plan-or-simulate-execution loop the designer is able to change the situation description or goal so as to produce the situation-action rules which are desired as the basic knowledge of the agent prior to it its actual embedding in the domain. This off-line simulation of the agent's performance not only extends the basic knowledge of the system, it also allows the designer to check the adequacy and extent of the agent's existing situation-action rule set.

---

[4] It is this feature that forces us to insist that all consequences of an action are stored in a TEST operator description. If we relax this assumption, then the way in which we simulate the effect of performing an action needs to change. One possibility is to adopt the techniques described in Ginsberg and Smith (1987). Given a description of a situation, the idea is to add the consequences of the performed action. The resulting situation description may then be inconsistent. Consistency is then restored by deleting as few propositions as possible. If we were to adopt this approach, then the user would be given greater flexibility in formalizing problems in TEST. The cost would be greater inefficiency during the generation of situated-action rules.

The question of how much basic knowledge should be given to the agent is a matter for the designer's discretion. Obviously, the more 'canned' plans the agent begins with, the better its initial performance will be but our intention is not that all problem-solving activity be done for the agent prior to its embedding. As a rough heuristic, the more dynamic the execution domain is, the more pre-planning will be needed for acceptable agent performance.

However, no matter how much effort the designer puts into designing a complete set of situation-action rules, it is likely that for more complex applications the set of rules will be incomplete. This raises the question how the agent should decide its response when faced with a novel situation in a potentially time-critical situation. Three basic strategies are possible, all of which have been implemented in our architecture. Which strategy is used is determined by the global variable *decision-tactic*.

The first strategy, *Full-planning*, is as follows: simply invoke TEST with the current situation description and the overall agent goal. This strategy is the most time-consuming of the three but delivers a plan from which the derived situation-action rules are guaranteed to achieve the goal in an optimal number of steps. Most classical planners implicitly use this strategy. It is most appropriate in cases where decision-making is not time-critical i.e. for off-line planning or in essentially static domains.

Partial-planning provides an alternative strategy: find the situation-action rule for the goal whose situation description is 'closest' to the actual situation. As a simple heuristic the 'closest' might be defined as the rule whose situation description has the most predicates that are the same as the actual situation. TEST is then invoked to plan to transform the actual situation into this nearest situation (by making the predicates which differ between the situations the same). This should reduce planning time and the resultant situation-action rules will still advance the agent towards its goal. However, unlike full-planning, this strategy does not guarantee an optimal solution (although, give a sufficiently powerful specification in TEST, we are guaranteed that one will be found). After all, there might be a more direct route from the present situation to the goal situation than via the situation described in the 'closest' situation-action rule. The partial-planning strategy bears some resemblance to the re-planning facilities in SIPE. It might be used in cases where time-criticality is a factor in problem solving but 'instant' decisions are not needed. Thus it seems suitable for moderately dynamic domains.

The final possibility is *Guess-an-action*. Under this strategy, an action which is applicable in the current situation is selected at random and then executed. Our current implementation achieves this by the use of "filters" which detect whether an operator is generally applicable to a situation, and "binders" which instantiate the argument(s) of the operator to yield the selected action[5]. The filters associated with an operator are generated automatically from the assumptions that are stored in the TEST assumption pool: They correspond to the preconditions associated with an action. The guess-an-action strategy is the least expensive computationally. However, there is no guarantee that the selected

---

[5] For later versions of SITACT, we are hoping to find a more "intelligent" guessing strategy than the entirely random action selection method used at present.

action has any utility in achieving the goal, and under certain circumstances it may even render the goal unachievable. This strategy is thus very similar to Drummond's strategy of allowing the execution module to select actions directly from the plan net before full planning has been completed. The guess-an-action strategy is most useful for highly time-critical situations and is based on the principle that in emergencies it is better to make an 'intelligent guess' about the action to perform rather than simply doing nothing. It is thus suitable for highly dynamic domains but at the cost of impaired agent performance in comparison to the other two methods.

Obviously, the previous basic strategies can be combined to form a more sophisticated hybrid strategy, namely *Guess-then-try-to-plan*. As in the *guess-an-action* strategy, a random action is selected. This action is then scheduled for execution but not actually executed. Partial-planning is then began but with the additional proviso that it can be interrupted and the scheduled action executed should the available time for decision-making be exceeded. This strategy can be generalized further, so that after partial-planning has been completed, and no need to act has been detected, the system may engage in full planning, again with the proviso that this process may be interrupted. This strategy seems to offer an optimal compromise in the performance-decision speed trade-off and is thus appropriate to domains of any degree of dynamism.

5   Limitations and future work

The main limitation in the present implementation is the status of the bottom most level. The actions generated by SITACT are too high-level to be used directly to guide a robot. Moreover, the perceptual inputs that SITACT expects are high-level and it is not clear to what extent it is realistic to expect such descriptions to be forthcoming.

One possible solution is to adopt techniques developed by Malcolm and Smithers (1990). They describe a system that is capable of constructing relatively complicated assemblies. The plan execution agent is based on the notion of a behavioural module. A behavioural module accomplishes useful motions of parts. The assembly planner communicates to the plan execution agent in terms of behavioural modules. Thus, the assembly planner does not have to plan in terms of robotic joint movements, it can plan in terms of movement of blocks from one position to another.

The attraction of Malcolm's and Smither's system lies in the fact that the language in which the planner communicates with the plan execution agent, which clearly corresponds to the lowest level in our architecture, is high-level. In fact, if Malcolm and Smither's proposal is correct, then the action descriptions that are generated by SITACT are at the right level. However, there are a number of open problems with the notion of behavioural module. For example, the behavioural module is responsible for fixing problems that arise during plan execution. For example, consider the following situation. SITACT has called the behavioural module responsible for picking up block *a*. However, since *a* is covered in green soap, it slides out of the robot's gripper. It is the behavioural module that is then responsible for re-trying the pick-up action. It seems to us that there might be situations in which this constrains the architecture too much. While it is clear than certain minor problems that arise during execution could (and should) be fixed by behavioural modules, such as small misalignments, more major problems, such as a block not being held, are perhaps more appropriately dealt with by SITACT. It is also not entirely clear how behavioural modules can be used at the perception side.

Further limitations arise because SITACT assumes that TEST delivers only the simplest type of plans, namely linearized plans for single goals which allow only one action to be executed at a time. This raises the issue what modifications would be needed to the SITACT module to ensure that it could deal with more complicated plans. In particular, how could it deal with conjunctive goals and parallel actions?

The main problem that arises when we consider conjunctive goals is whether the module should hold situation-action rules for conjunctive goals or individual goals which would be sequentially executed to achieve the desired conjunction. The first method is wasteful of storage space. Moreover, it requires that the agent do more plan generation since even if a complete set of situation-action rules exists to achieve each goal separately the agent will have to plan to achieve the conjunction of the goals. However, the second method has the problem that the situation-action rules to achieve the individual goals may interact to prevent their conjunction being achieved. One might imagine using some form of goal scheduler which employs domain knowledge to select the order in which the the agent tries to achieve the individual goals, but there is still no guarantee that the rules for each goal have not been derived in such a way that they 'clobber' each other regardless of ordering. To avoid this problem we initially at least intend to store rules for conjunctive goals. This is also in accord with our desire to keep most of the 'intelligence' of the agent at the TEST level during the early development of our architecture.

Another desirable generalization would be to allow for parallel actions in SITACT. This is more problematic because of the STRIPS-like operator effect templates used during rule derivation. Parallel actions which do not interact (in the sense that they do not change the same predicates in a situation description) are allowable but those which do interact are not. Thus, consider a blocks-world using two robot arms. The SITACT module could cope with each hand placing a block on the table simultaneously but could not deal with the held blocks being brought together simultaneously to form a stack, because in the latter case whether the bottom block was described as clear or not would depend on which operator effect template was invoked first. Hence, unless a radically different method of rule derivation is used, our architecture is forced to restrict itself in the cases of parallel action it allows.

Another issue that arises is that of deriving situation-action rules from TEST-generated plans that are more generally applicable than for simply achieving the top-level agent goal. At the moment, all the situation-action rules created from a TEST-generated plan are indexed under the goal that was originally passed to TEST. They will therefore only be used if the system is faced with exactly the same top-level goal. However, often situation-action rules are more generally applicable. For example, consider a plan to stack a on b

by removing c from a, removing d from b, picking up a, and finally putting a on b. It is clear that this plan contains actions which achieve the subgoal of clearing a, the subgoal of clearing b, and the subgoal of moving a to b. Currently, however, all situation-action rules derived from such a plan would be stored together under the banner of 'Achieve-a-on-b'. By decomposing this rule set into its subgoals, the situation-action rules would become employable for different top-level goals and one avoids the redundant storage of the same rules for these different goals, a problem which would become particularly acute when conjunctive goals are stored.

A final shortcoming of the present implementation is that the situation-action rules that SITACT generates are in a sense too specific. In the derivation of such rules, we take the entire state of world before the action occurred as our situation. However, certain facts are clearly irrelevant to the situation-action rule. Thus, as long as a and b are clear, the question whether c is clear or not is irrelevant to the rule for stacking a on b. We therefore need to restrict the information about the world that is used to build situation-action rules. Note however that finding the appropriate definition of irrelevance is not straightforward. In particular, an initial suggestion that the only relevant facts in the world are those that are explicitly referred to in the current action is unsatisfactory. For example, even though the assumption in TEST concerning picking up a only refers to whether a is clear and whether the hand is free, if the goal is stacking a on b, the question whether b is clear or not is clearly relevant: when b is not clear, picking up a is not a smart thing to do; one first wants to remove whatever is on top of b.

6 Conclusion

We have presented an architecture for the construction of autonomous agents functioning in dynamic domains. It employs classical planning as a declarative problem-solving method integrated with situation-action rules as the 'compiled' results of this planning. We argue that the architecture provides the agent with the reactivity needed in time-critical situations. On the other hand, it is also flexible enough that it allows the designer to provide the agent with the basic knowledge necessary to function in a domain prior to its actual embedding.

References

Agre, P. (1988) The Dynamic Structure of Everyday Life, Technical Report 1085, Dept. of Comp. Sci., MIT

Agre, P. & Chapman, D. (1987) Pengi : An Implementation of a Theory of Activity, *AAAI-6*, 268-272

Agre, P. & Chapman, D. (1988) What are Plans for ?, A.I. Memo 1050, Dept. of Comp. Sci., MIT

Allen, J. (1984) Towards a general theory of action and time. *Artificial Intelligence*, 23, 123-54.

Ambros-Ingerson, J.A. (1986) Relationships Between Planning and Execution, CSCM-25, Dept. of Comp. Sci., Essex University

Ambros-Ingerson, J.A. & Steel, S. (1988) Integrating Planning, Execution and Monitoring, *AAAI-7*, 83-88

Chapman, D. & Agre, P. (1986) Abstract Reasoning as Emergent from Concrete Activity, *Proc. 1986 Workshop on Reasoning about Actions and Plans*, 411-424

Chapman, D. (1987) Planning for Conjunctive Goals, *Artificial Intelligence*, 32, 333-377

Drummond, M. (1989) Situated Control Rules, *Proc. 1st International Conference on Principles of Knowledge Representation and Reasoning*, 103-113

Elfrink, B. & Reichgelt, H. (1989) Assertion-time inference in logic-based systems Jackson, P., Reichgelt, H. & van Harmelen, F. (eds.) *Logic-Based Knowledge Representation*. MIT Press

Firby, R.J. (1987) An Investigation into Reactive Planning in Complex Domains, *AAAI-6*, 202-206

Georgeff, M.P. & Lansky, A. (1987) Reactive Reasoning and Planning, *AAAI-6*, 677-682

Ginsberg, M & Smith, D. (1987) Reasoning about action I: A possible worlds approach. In F. Brown (ed) *The frame problem in Artificial Intelligence* Morgan Kaufmann.

Israel, D. (1980) What's wrong with non-monotonic logic. *AAAI-80*, 99-101.

Levesque H.J. & Brachman R.J. (1985) A Fundamental Tradeoff in Knowledge Representation and Reasoning. In R. Brachman & H. Levesque (eds.) *Readings in Knowledge Representation*, Morgan Kaufmann

Malcolm, M. & Smithers, T. (1990) Symbol grounding via a hybrid architecture in an autonomous assembly system. *Robotics and Autonomous Systems*, 6, 123-144.

Reichgelt, H. (1988) The place of defaults in a reasoning system. In B. Smith & G. Kelleher *Reason maintenance systems and their applications*. Ellis-Horwood.

Reichgelt, H. & Shadbolt, N. (1989) Planning as theory extension. *AISB-7*, 191-201.

Reichgelt, H. & Shadbolt, N. (1990) A specification tool for planning systems. *ECAI-9*, 541-546.

Rosenschein, S.J. (1985) Formal Theories of Knowledge in AI and Robotics, Technical Note 362, SRI International

Russell S.J. (1989) Execution Architectures and Compilation *IJCAI-11*, 15-20

Schoppers, M.J. (1987) Universal Plans for Reactive Robots in Unpredictable Environments, *IJCAI-10*, 1039-1046

Wilkins, D.E. (1985) Recovering from Execution Errors in SIPE, *Computational Intelligence*, 1, 33-45

Wilkins, D.E. (1988) *Practical Planning : Extending the Classical AI Planning Paradigm*, Morgan Kaufmann

Associating A.I. Planner Entities with an underlying Time Point Network

Brian Drabble and Richard Kirby
Artificial Intelligence Applications Institute
University of Edinburgh
Edinburgh EH1 1HN

Abstract

This article outlines the design rationale behind the entity and time representation and reasoning system incorporated into the O-PLAN2 planner. The paper shows the advantages of splitting the planning entities (such as activities, events and time orderings) from the underlying temporal information of the domain. This allows a single architecture to be tailored to act as planner, scheduler or controller with only minor changes in the knowledge required. The paper concludes with a description of the current O-PLAN2 system together with our early results and future research direction.

1 Background to the Research

The earlier O-PLAN project at Edinburgh [2], 1984-1988, focussed on the techniques and technologies necessary to support the informed search processes needed to generate predictive plans for subsequent execution by some agent. The current O-PLAN2 [1] project continues the emphasis placed on the formal design of a Planning Architecture in identifying the modular functionality, the roles of these modules, and their software interfaces.

O-PLAN2 is incorporated within a blackboard-like framework; for efficiency reasons we have chosen an agenda driven architecture. Items on the agendas represent outstanding tasks to be performed during the planning process, and they relate directly to the set of *flaws* identified as existing within any non-final state of the emerging plan. A simple example of a *flaw* is that of a condition awaiting satisfaction, or an action requiring refinement to a lower level. An agenda controller will choose on each planning cycle which flaw to operate on next.

[1]This research is supported by the US Air Force/European Office of Aerospace Research and Development by grant number EOARD/88-0044 monitored by Dr Nort Fowler at the Rome Air Development Centre

2   Architecture

A generalised picture of the architecture is shown in figure 1. The main components are:

The Domain Information. Domain descriptions will be supplied to O-PLAN2 in a structured language, which will be compiled into the internal data static structures to be used during planning. The description will include details of actions which can be performed in the domain, goals to describe the planning requirements, and incremental updates or re-specifications of knowledge sources. The structured language (we call it Task Formalism) is the means through which a domain writer or domain expert can supply the domain specific information to the O-PLAN2 system, which itself is a domain *independent* planner. O-PLAN2 will embody many search space pruning mechanisms (strong search methods) and will fall back on other weak methods, if these fail, in order to preserve completeness of the search space. The task formalism is the mechanism that enables the user of the system to supply his domain dependent knowledge to assist the system in its search. This information is not updated by the operation of the system, so the information flow is depicted outwards from this static data block to show the support offered to the functional modules.

The Plan State. In contrast to the static information outlined above, the plan state (on the left of the figure) is the dynamic data structures used during planning and houses the emerging plan. There are many components to this structure, the principal ones being:

- the plan itself. This is based on a partial order of activities, as originally suggested by the NOAH planner. In O-PLAN2 the plan information is concentrated in the "Associated Data Structure" (ADS). The ADS is a list of node and link structures noting temporal and resource information (indirectly), plan information and a planning history.

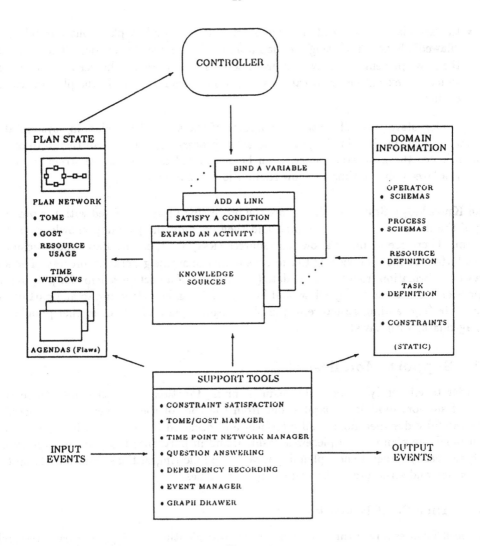

Figure 1

- the plan rationale. Borrowing from Nonlin and O-PLAN, the system keeps explicit information to "explain" why the plan is built the way it is. This rationale is called the Goal Structure and, along with the Table of Multiple Effects (GOST and TOME), provides an efficient data structure for the underlying condition achievement procedure used in O-PLAN2 (c.f. Chapman's Modal Truth Criteria [1]).

- the agenda list(s). O-PLAN2 will start with a complete plan, but one which is "flawed", hence preventing the plan from being capable of execution. The nature of the flaws present will be varied, from actions which are at a higher level than that which the executing agent can operate, to linkages necessary in the plan to resolve conflict.

The plan state is a self-contained snapshot of the state of the planning system at a particular point in time in the plan generation process. It contains all the state of the system hence the generation process can be suspended and this single structure rolled back at a later point in time to allow resumption of the search[2].

The Knowledge Sources. These are the processing units associated with the processing of the flaws contained in the plan and they embody the planning knowledge of the system. There are as many knowledge sources (KSs) are there are flaw types, including the interface to the user wishing to exert his influence on the generation process. The KSs draw on information from the static data (*e.g.* the use of an action schema for purposes of expansion) to process a single flaw, and in turn they can add structure to any part of the plan state (*e.g.* adding structure to the plan, inserting new effects or further populating the agenda(s) with flaws).

2.1 Support Modules.

In order to efficiently support the main planning functionality in O-PLAN2 there is a layer of support modules separated out from the core of the planner. These modules have carefully designed functional interfaces and declared function in order that we can both build the planner in a piecewise fashion, and in particular that we can experiment with and easily integrate new planning ideas. The following sections defines in detail the motivation and structure of the main support modules.

2.1.1 Time Point Network (TPN)

The need for a separate time network system was identified during the earlier research programme for O-PLAN. O-PLAN's ability to represent the delays between actions and to interact with events occurring in the real world relied on data structures which were considered inefficient and cumbersome. O-PLAN could interact with fixed events such as the delivery of a resource but could not handle dynamic events occurring in the target domain. The delays between actions were handled by incorporating delays for each arch leaving a node which made the representation inflexible and inefficient.

---

[2]Actually this assumes that the task formalism and the knowledge sources used on re-start are the same "static" information used previously.

A separate time representation scheme will allow a speed up in operations such as Question Answering (QA) and Temporal Coherence (TC) and will allow plan structures based on different temporal constructs, *i.e.* points, intervals and events. The time representation scheme needs to represent a variety of information which includes:

- The ability to represent actions and events from some given absolute beginning of time. This can be relative to the time of planning, execution or some known external events.

- The temporal constraints which limit the "position" in time at which an action or event can occur and will be represented as a upper and lower value pair. The action of events constraint will be specified relative to absolute beginning of time or relative to some other action or event.

- The dependency information which create a "belief" for the continued existence of an action or event within the plan.

- The creation of a time-line which contains those actions and events which have known start time (*i.e.* the lower and upper values are the same). This will allow easy comparison of actions and events as well as aid in the analysis of resources used during a plan execution.

2.1.2   Time Network data structures

The choice of which temporal construct to use as the basic building block was a very important consideration to be made. It was decided to use a *point based* construct for several reasons, these being:

- A time point representation directly supports standard Operational Research/PERT type algorithms.

- If a knowledge source requires to reason about the plan state in terms of intervals these can be recovered from a point based network However, points cannot be recovered from an interval based representation.

- Constraint satisfaction algorithms already exist which can operate efficiently on a point based network.

The data structures which are used to implement the temporal point network (TPN) will now be described.

2.1.3 Time point network

The time point network consists of a set of points each of which has an upper and lower bound on its temporal distance from the start of time. The format of each point is as follows:

```
(pt<n> lower_bound upper_bound)
```

The points will be associated with actions, links and events, but this association will only be made at the Associated Data Structure (ADS) level. The point number is used as the index giving a constant retrieval time for any number of points. This structure will allow points to be retrieved, deleted and compared easily with a minimum of overhead. Points in this network which have an upper and lower bound the same will be marked with a tag so that they can easily be retrieved from the landmark line (Section 2.1.6)

In later versions of the TPN it my be possible to contextually divide the points of the TPN according to their *type* or *use*. The resource reasoning modules in QA for example may require only those points involving resources creation, deletion or usage. This may also apply to the world model and execution reasoning modules within O-PLAN2. This would be an extra level of context information between the Associated Data Structure and the information held in the "clouds" of effect format.

2.1.4 Managerial constraints

The *managerial* constraints are used by the TPN to handle explicit constraints between points within the network. For example the begin point and end points of an action must be constrained to be equal to the lower and upper values of its duration. The managerial constraints are also used to handle user specified constraints such as:

- The start time of one action being a prescribed distance before the start of another. For example, if our plan contains a sensing action then we would like the sensing action to begin a certain time after the action to be sensed has begun. This allows us to check that the action is progressing and that the required effects are now in present in the real world. The term "Action Progression" is used to describe this situation.

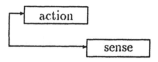

- The finish time of one action being a prescribed distance before or after the finish time of another. An example of this comes from a steel rolling plant domain. Here the user does not know the time taken to roll the steel or heat the steel but the user does require the end of the heating phase to be as close as possible to the end of the previous rolling phase. The term "Action Continuity" is used to describe this sort of situation.

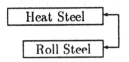

A problem which may arise when using managerial links is that of loops occurring with the TPN. To avoid this, checking will be performed when a new managerial constraint is added. A managerial link will be maintained by a dependency check that the temporal distance between two points is maintained, *i.e.* it lies between the links upper and lower values. The managerial links will add greater flexibility to the representation by allowing points with no explicit positional constraints to be placed in time. In the following example

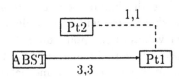

We can calculate on demand the position constraint for Pt2 by knowing the position constraint for Pt1 and the managerial constraint between Pt1 and Pt2. The adding of new positional constraints will only be done as the result of a request to the TPN and *not* in order to create a closure of all relations.

2.1.5 Position constraints

The positional constraints are used to fix a point in time by specifying an upper and lower bound on its temporal "distance" from some absolute time value ABST. The value of ABST can be either time of plan generation, plan execution or some external event the plan should create or avoid. If a constraint between two points is not specified then a default of $(0, \infty)$ is assumed. The constraints are held in a table format with the index mechanism provided by the point number. The format of the table entries is as follows;

$$< Point - number >< List - of - constraints >< Current - glb - and - lub >$$

The GLB specifies the greatest upper bound and the LUB specifies the least upper bound. This gives us the *intersection* of all constraints specified for a point. The list of constraints is further divided into those which are specified as positional constraints and those which are managerial constraints. Any positional constraints which are introduced as a result of using managerial constraint information will be specially marked so that if at a later date a positional constraint is added, then only the necessary conflicts will be identified. The access times for this table is linear and tests have been carried out on tables exceeding 500 points to check on the maximum retrieval time.

2.1.6 Landmark line

The landmark line contains those points which have an upper and lower value with the same value *i.e.* co-incident. The points are sorted into ascending order from left right. The landmark line allows:

- Points to be easily compared for relations such as before, after, etc.

- Resources which have known usage times can be profiled thus aiding the resources reasoning required within the planner.

When a point is inserted into the landmark line it is *not* kept as a separate entry elsewhere within TPN. The landmark line will carry a dependency check so that if at a later date the upper and lower values of the point differ the point can be removed from the landmark line and reinstated as a point in the TPN. For example, if I change my mind about going shopping from 9.00am to sometime between 9.00am and 9.30am the corresponding end point will have to be removed from the landmark line. Each point in the land mark line is unique in that no two points can have exactly the same upper and lower values and be equal. If such a condition occurs then the points are unified and a message is sent to the ADS to inform it of the change which has been made. The use of the landmark line for resource management will have to be carefully investigated as only those resources requirements with exactly known times of occurrence. *i.e.* GLB = LUB will be entered there. Times which do not have this relation will have to be reasoned about in a similar way to that used in the EXCALIBUR system [3]

2.1.7 Time Network Manager (TNM)

The TMM is the collection of routines which interface the TPN to the ADS. These routines query the network and maintain its integrity in response to queries from the ADS. The main routines of the TNM consists of;

- **Query Routines** Checks whether a given action or constraint can be asserted in the TPN. Any failures are reported back to calling modules for its consideration

- Add or delete a point from the TPN

- Add or delete a constraint from the TPN

- **Constraint propagation and checking** Checks that a new constraint does not cause a violation within the current TPN.

2.2 Associated Data Structure (ADS)

The ADS provides the *contextual* information used to attach meaning to the contents of the TPN, and the data defining the emerging plan. The main elements of the plan are nodes and links, with ordering information as necessary to define the partial order relationships between these elements. The links between the actions and events of the plan are themselves held as nodes. This allows us to represent delays between actions cleanly and means that the reasoning mechanism does not have to decide between links and actions/events. Higher level support modules (such as QA, TOME and GOST Management (TGM), *etc.*) will rely heavily on the detail held in the ADS and on the functionality provided by the TPN. The ADS consists of information held in *two* different parts of the planner, namely the plan network (held within the Plan Manager (PM)) and the TOME and GOST entries (held within the TOME and GOST manager TGM). Figure 2 describes the relationships and data flow paths between the ADS and the TPN. The plan manager holds the graph of action, events and dummies which are in the "current plan", as well as the symbolic time constraints. These symbolic constraints are computed as metric time positional constraints or managerial constraints within the TPN.

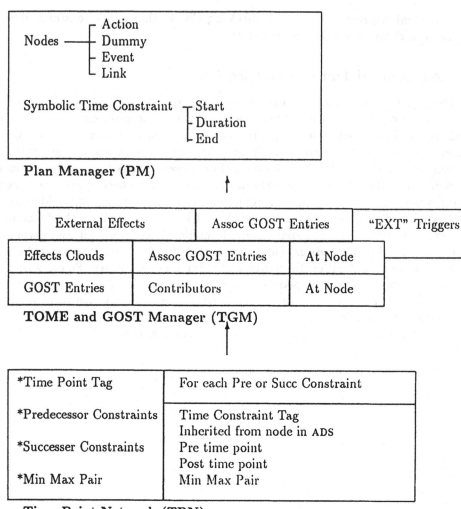

Plan Manager (PM)

TOME and GOST Manager (TGM)

Time Point Network (TPN)

Figure 2.

The TOME and GOST Manager handles both plan effects required within the plan and external effects occurring in the real world which are also required within the plan. The entries of the TOME and GOST are partitioned into those requiring external events and those satisfied from within the plan. This is because the external events will in most cases have *triggering* conditions which must be met for the event to occur. For example, the bank opening at 9.30am requires no triggers where as a kettle boiling will require external and internal (to the plan) triggers such as the kettle being plugged in and the plug being switched on. External information will be provided and maintained by the World Model

Manager (WMM) from a qualitative model built up as the plan is being generated. As O-PLAN2 develops for use in continuous command and control applications the need to predict and recover from situations becomes much more demanding. The earlier work of Drabble [3] will provide a focus for how this will be achieved. The idea behind this form of control is that shallow reasoning such as TC [4] will need to be increased with deeper models in more complex domains. The different ways we envision using qualitative reasoning are as follows:

1. If an aircraft has problems with its hydraulics then it would be a good idea to place the flaps down and lock the undercarriage before carrying out any further planning.

2. The qualitative model may also be used for generating extra constraints between actions of the plan due to newly discovered interactions. For example in making steel try to have the finish of the heating process as close to the rolling as possible.

3. During execution of a plan the qualitative reasoning can be used to check for

   (a) the unexpected side effects of actions
   (b) undesirable changes/events occurring within the domain
   (c) the successful outcome of a set of plan actions whose collective effects are designed to bring about a change in the domain.

3   Summary

The O-PLAN project took an architectural approach to the problem of representing decision making within a planning system. O-PLAN2 goes further in that it attempts to split the representation components required in the decision making processes identified. The advantages of this approach have been outlined in the paper. The first version of the TPN and ADS has been implemented and tested. These tests involved creating networks of points in excess of 2000 points with a constraint set in access of 1500. This has provided us with timing information for plan networks of the order of 300 nodes which is the maximum size of problem we wish to tackle with early versions of O-PLAN2. Further research is continuing on the partitioning of the network and in the dependency/triggering required for the knowledge sources and World Model Manager.

References

[1] Chapman, D. Planning for conjunctive goals. *Artificial Intelligence Vol. 32, pp. 333-377, 1987.*

[2] Currie, K. & Tate, A. O-Plan: the Open Planning Architecture. *To appear in the AI Journal. Also* AIAI-TR-*67. 1989.*

[3] Drabble, B. Planning and reasoning with processes. *Procs. of the 8th Workshop of the Alvey Planning* SIG, *The Institute of Electrical Engineers, November, 1988.*

[4] Drummond, M. & Currie, K. Exploiting temporal coherence in nonlinear plan construction. *Procs. of* IJCAI-*89, Detroit.*

[5] Hayes-Roth, B. & Hayes-Roth, F. A cognitive model of planning. *Cognitive Science, pp 275 to 310, 1979.*

[6] McDermott, D.V. A Temporal Logic for Reasoning about Processes and Plans In *Cognitive Science, 6, pp 101-155, 1978.*

[7] Sacerdoti, E. A structure for plans and behaviours. *Artificial Intelligence series, publ. North Holland, 1977.*

[8] Stefik, M. Planning with constraints. In *Artificial Intelligence, Vol. 16, pp. 111-140. 1981.*

[9] Tate, A. Generating project networks. *In procs.* IJCAI-77, *1977.*

[10] Vere, S. Planning in time: windows and durations for activities and goals. IEEE *Transactions on Pattern Analysis and Machine Intelligence Vol. 5, 1981.*

[11] Wilkins, D. Practical Planning. *Morgan Kaufman, 1988.*

DEFAULT CONNECTIONS
IN A MODAL PLANNING FRAMEWORK

Bertram Fronhöfer

Institut für Informatik, Technische Universität München
Arcisstr. 21, Postfach 20 24 20, D–8000 München 2, West Germany
fronhoef@lan.informatik.tu-muenchen.dpb.de

Keywords
logics for plan generation, application of modal logic, frame problem.

ABSTRACT

We present a framework for plan generation based on rather ordinary modal logic. To overcome the frame problem which is due to the monotonicity of traditional logic, this framework is enhanced by a particular kind of "default reasoning", which is enabled by the particular way we have chosen to specify plan generation problems. We claim that the proposed framework translates the essential ideas of linear proofs [BIB 86b] into modal logic.

0. INTRODUCTION

A very natural logical view of plan generation is to understand it as the task of deriving a certain goal situation from a given initial situation and from the specification of a set of permitted actions. Briefly stated, due to the monotonicity of logic all approaches conceived along this view laboured under the so–called frame problem, i.e. the necessity to carry out a lot of reasoning by so–called frame axioms in order to establish which facts of a situation remain valid after the application of an action. (Note that this problem could neither be completely overcome through the use of non-monotonic logics, because there the frame axioms were just replaced by axioms stating that facts survive if they are not abnormal. The necessary amount of reasoning remains roughly the same.)

In the present paper we formulate a class of plan generation problems in modal logic, which naturally suffers form the forementioned drawbacks. At first sight, our framework looks even less attractive than the logical approaches proposed in the past, but—as we will show—our formulation permits a technique to shortcut proofs, such that frame axioms are not needed in general.

The plan of the paper is as follows:

Section 1 introduces the basic ideas of the paper by means of an example of a plan generation problem in a blocks world. Section 2 gives a detailed presentation of the modal planning framework. As far as developed in this section, it is an absolutely conventional application of modal logic to plan generation, which relies completely on frame axioms. Section 3 develops a kind of default reasoning—different from the existing ones—based on syntactic criteria of deductions. By means of this default non–reasoning we are able to perform a kind of shortcut during the proof process, which makes the frame axioms superfluous. Section 4 presents some plan generation problems which the system thus far developed cannot cope with. Section 5 elaborates extensions of the modal planning framework to overcome these limitations. Finally, in the conclusion we compare the ideas presented here with the approach to plan generation via linear proofs (see [BIB 86b]) which was an important source of inspiration for the present work.

1. A MOTIVATING EXAMPLE

Modal logic—the logic of possibility and necessity—is traditionally interpreted over a set of worlds. Assuming these worlds to be somewhat similar, i.e. sharing their objects and a common interest in these objects' properties, we can also speak about different situations of the same world or universe.

A field of application which has to deal with changing situations of a world is planning or plan generation in robot problem solving: Here the operating of a robot brings about new situations of a world from earlier produced or originally given situations. That there is a situation in the context of plan generation in which a certain formula $\mathcal{F}$ is valid, can be viewed in the context of modal logic as that exists a world (accessible from the given one) in which $\mathcal{F}$ is valid. The latter statement can be expressed as $\Diamond\mathcal{F}$, which is read as "$\mathcal{F}$ is possible".

This analogy can be exploited to express plan generation problems in ordinary modal logic, which we wish to illustrate by a small blocks world example taken from [BIB 86b] and [FRO 87] , where a block b is moved from the top of a block a down on the table.

We start from a situation where a block a is on a table: T(a), a block b is on top of a : O(b, a), the top of b is clear: C(b) and the robot's hand is empty: E. Since this is the initial situation— hence an obviously existing one—it can be translated to modal logic as that exists a certain world in which these facts are valid, which is formalized as

$$\Diamond\Big(\mathsf{T(a)} \land \mathsf{O(b,a)} \land \mathsf{C(b)} \land \mathsf{E}\Big) \qquad (I)$$

To generate a new situation from an existing one, the robot has to execute a particular action. Developing further an intuition from [BIB 86b], these actions can be specified by rules which are basically of implicative form : antecedent $\longrightarrow$ consequent

- The antecedent shall comprise all facts of the existing situation which are involved in the action—either as being necessary conditions for the action's application or as being facts which will be false after the action has been carried out.

- The consequent conveys that a new situation can come to exist—that there is another possible world—which is described by a set of facts to be valid in this new situation. These facts are either newly created by the action or are facts which were involved as preconditions in the action, but are not affected by it.

Since these rules shall be applicable to every situation, they must be valid in each possible world, i.e. they are necessary.

In the case of our example the robot must be able to pick up a block from the top of another one and be able to put a block down on the table. These two actions are described by the following rules:

$$\Box\forall x, y \Big(\mathsf{E} \land \mathsf{C}(x) \land \mathsf{O}(x,y) \longrightarrow \Diamond\big(\mathsf{H}(x) \land \mathsf{C}(y)\big)\Big) \qquad (R_1)$$
$$\Box\forall v \Big(\mathsf{H}(v) \longrightarrow \Diamond\big(\mathsf{E} \land \mathsf{T}(v)\big)\Big) \qquad (R_2)$$

(R_1) can be read:
if we are in a situation (or possible world) where the robot's hand is empty and the top of a block x is clear and x is on a block y, then there exists a situation (or is accessible a possible world) in which the robot holds block x in his hand and the top of block y is clear.

(R_2) can be read:
if we are in a situation (or possible world) where the robot holds block v, then there exists a situation (or is accessible a possible world) in which the robot's hand is empty and v is on the table.

A goal of a plan generation problem asks for the existence of a situation which is partially specified by a set of facts, i.e. the existence of a particular possible world. This means for our example that we want to derive the formula

$$\Diamond(T(b) \wedge T(a) \wedge E) \qquad (G)$$

which reads, that we are asking for a situation in which the blocks a and b are both on the table and the robot's hand is empty.

As a first attempt we could summarize the formal presentation of our problem as the task to prove the formula $I \wedge R_1 \wedge R_2 \longrightarrow G$ or

$$\Diamond(T(a) \wedge O(b,a) \wedge C(b) \wedge E)$$
$$\wedge \left(\Box \forall x, y \, (E \wedge C(x) \wedge O(x,y) \longrightarrow \Diamond(H(x) \wedge C(y))) \right)$$
$$\wedge \left(\Box \forall v \, (H(v) \longrightarrow \Diamond(E \wedge T(v))) \right)$$
$$\longrightarrow \Diamond(T(b) \wedge T(a) \wedge E)$$

Unfortunately, this formula is not provable—we fail in the attempt to deduce that $T(a)$ is still valid in the goal situation—which must be remedied by adding appropriate frame axioms. (The frame axioms which facts are not affected by the action and are consequently still valid in the following situation. Note that all facts which change are dealt with in the rule itsself according to the specification philosophy explained above.)

Remark: Readers familiar with [BIB 86b] or [FRO 87] will notice the strong resemblance of the above formulation to the one shown in these papers. That the corresponding formula there is provable, but not ours, is due to the modal operator $\Diamond$: while we can deduce $\mathcal{A} \wedge \mathcal{B}$, if $\mathcal{A}$ and $\mathcal{B}$ are given, we cannot deduce $\Diamond(\mathcal{A} \wedge \mathcal{B})$ from $\Diamond\mathcal{A}$ and $\Diamond\mathcal{B}$. ∎

The frame axioms needed in our approach are bulky and plentiful. They do not only deal with single facts, but with arbitrary combinations of these. Their size is further increased by the fact, that they are hierarchically ordered extensions of the rules, and thus are indeed replacing them. Our frame axioms say intuitively, that if a set of facts is valid in a situation which also satisfies the antecedent of a certain rule, then these facts will also be valid in the world brought about by the corresponding action, iff these facts are different from the facts in the antecedent of that rule.

In our example we have to shift the fact $T(a)$ along the actions to the goal situation. Since this literal is different from the facts in the antecedent of our rules, we can obtain the following two frame axioms by extending these rules:

$$\Box \forall x, y \left(T(a) \wedge E \wedge C(x) \wedge O(x,y) \longrightarrow \Diamond(T(a) \wedge H(x) \wedge C(y)) \right) \qquad (F_1)$$
$$\Box \forall v \left(T(a) \wedge H(v) \longrightarrow \Diamond(T(a) \wedge E \wedge T(v)) \right) \qquad (F_2)$$

Taking these frame axioms instead of the original rules, we can now derive the goal formula, thus proving the existence of a plan. Having accomplished the proof, the plan is presented in the world–path which gives access to the facts of the goal formula. We will come back to this example in the next section, where we will also show a proof of the goal derivation.

2. A PRIMITIVE MODAL PLANNING LOGIC

After the intuitive introduction of the preceding section we will now give a precise definition of our modal framework for plan generation.

As a basis we assume the ordinary language of first–order logic which we extend by the usual modal operators $\Diamond$(**possibility**) and $\Box$(**necessity**), which are related by $\neg\Diamond\mathcal{F} \leftrightarrow \Box\neg\mathcal{F}$. In addition, the accessibility relation is required to be transitive. Furthermore, we assume that names do not change reference from one world to the other.

To specify planning problems, we will have to speak about situations. We assume a **situation** to be indicated by a set of positive facts which are true in this situation. Such a (generally incomplete) description—or partial representation of a situation—corresponds formally to a set of **unnegated** literals $L_1, \ldots, L_n$.

Definition :
A **plan generation problem** is specified through 3 components:

- The **initial situation** given by a set of facts $F_1, \ldots, F_n$.
  We postulate existence of the initial situation by affirming that the conjunction of these facts is possible, i.e. we take

  $$\Diamond \forall \overline{x_I} (F_1 \wedge \ldots \wedge F_n) \qquad (I)$$

  as an axiom of our system. ($\overline{x_I}$ is the list of all variables occurring in $F_1, \ldots, F_n$.)

- The **goal**, also given by a set of facts, say $G_1, \ldots, G_k$, indicates a situation, the existence of which we want to prove, i.e. the possibility of their conjunction :

  $$\Diamond \exists \overline{x_G} (G_1 \wedge \ldots \wedge G_k) \qquad (G)$$

  This formula is considered a theorem to be proved from the axioms.
  ($\overline{x_G}$ is the list of all variables occurring in $G_1, \ldots, G_k$.)

- The remaining axioms which are needed are the **rules** and **frame axioms**. The rules, which formalize the actions of a robot, convey that if a certain set of facts $A_1, \ldots, A_g$ is true in a particular situation, then we can conclude that a further situation specified by a set of facts $B_1, \ldots, B_h$ (potentially) exists. Such statements shall be valid ubiquitously, i.e. necessarily be true. Consequently we get

  $$\Box \forall \overline{x_R} \left(A_1 \wedge \ldots \wedge A_g \longrightarrow \Diamond(B_1 \wedge \ldots \wedge B_h) \right)$$

  ($\overline{x_R}$ is the list of all variables occurring in $A_1, \ldots, A_g$ or in $B_1, \ldots, B_h$.)

The frame axioms are very regular extensions of such a rule. They shall assure that each set of facts $C_1, \ldots, C_l$ which are independent from the $A_1, \ldots, A_g$ are also valid in the situation indicated by the $B_1, \ldots, B_h$. Thus we get

$$\Box \forall \overline{x_F} \left(C_1 \wedge \ldots \wedge C_l \wedge A_1 \wedge \ldots \wedge A_g \right.$$
$$\wedge \operatorname{INDEP}(C_1, \{A_1, \ldots, A_g\}) \wedge \ldots \wedge \operatorname{INDEP}(C_l, \{A_1, \ldots, A_g\})$$
$$\left. \longrightarrow \Diamond(C_1 \wedge \ldots \wedge C_l \wedge B_1 \wedge \ldots \wedge B_h) \right)$$

The symbol INDEP is a meta–predicate which must be replaced by respective axioms. Its meaning will depend on the application—the domain in which we plan and the type of robot—and on the way this application is represented.

Definition :

(1) A plan generation problem is **pure** iff the initial situation and the rules and frame axioms are its only axioms.

(2) A plan generation problem is **ground** iff
   - all literals of the initial situation are ground
   - for every rule the variables occurring in the consequent are a subset of the variables in the antecedent. ■

In case of a pure and ground plan generation problem independence may be reduced to different-ness, i.e. for all $i \in \{1,\ldots,l\}$ we replace $\text{INDEP}(C_i, \{A_1,\ldots,A_g\})$ by $C_i \not\equiv A_1 \wedge \ldots \wedge C_i \not\equiv A_g$. In this context $\equiv$ reduces to unifiable. If our plan generation problem is ground as well, INDEP may be implemented as being equivalent to failure of unification. At first sight this interpretation of independence might seem to be too primitive, but as a consequence of the philosophy that the antecedent of a rule should mention all facts which are in some way affected by the corresponding action, differentness will do as a guarantee of independence in most applications, at least where the STRIPS assumption holds.

Example :
Let us come back to the example from the introduction and show how it can be proved with a modal matrix proof method. (For a detailed presentation of modal proofs with the Connection Method see the technical report [FRO 89].) The first matrix without frame axioms shows the failure of unification of the literals $[\iota]T(a)$ and $[\nu]T(a)$ with $[\nu \leftarrow [\iota\,\lambda(x,y)\,\delta(v)]]$.

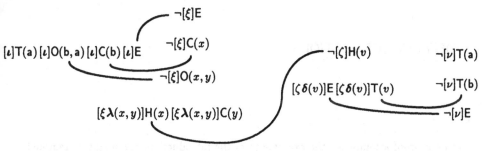

Explanations: The horizontal row of literals on the left denotes the initial situation, the two towers in the middle denote the two applied rules—the left one picks up the block b and the right one puts the block b down on the table—and finally, the column of atoms on the right describes the goal situation. The set of bows represents the spanning set of connections which makes the matrix complementary: this means that each 'horizontal line' traversing the matrix contains at least one connection.

In the next matrix the frame axioms stepwise deduce $[\iota\,\lambda(x,y)]T(a)$ and $[\iota\,\lambda(x,y)\,\delta(v)]T(a)$ as needed.

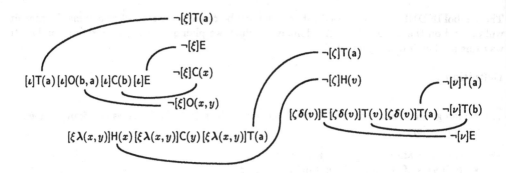

An abhorrent aspect of the system just defined is the great number of gigantic frame axioms. At first glance this seems to cause a further increase in inefficiency going even beyond the computational expenditure of classical situational calculus. However, due to the regular structure of our frame axioms we can generate the required frame axioms on request and this process can be performed by adding literals directly to the matrix. This allows us to implement our calculus equally efficiently (or equally inefficiently) as the situational calculus.

Summarizing this section, we can say that we presented a modal logic for planning which is heavily afflicted by the frame problem. We intend to relieve it from this burden by enhancing it with a suitable kind of default reasoning—or better, a default non–reasoning as we will expostulate in the sequel.

3. DEFAULT CONNECTIONS

During a proof attempt for the example from the introduction, one might be tempted to connect the literal $\neg[\iota\,\lambda(x,y)\,\delta(v)]T(a)$ directly with the literal $[\iota]T(a)$ of the initial situation; the only handicap precluding this connection is the incompatibility of the world–path. Intuitively spoken, what we want is that all those facts of a situation survive the application of an action, which are not involved in it, i.e. they should survive by default.

Disappointed by computational gains of default reasoning in the context of the frame problem, we plead for a way of reasoning which is distinguished by a minimal computational expenditure—essentially a default non–reasoning—relying on shortcuts during a proof process.

We intend to make such connections feasible through an appropriate generalization of the concept of connection; so–called default connections (based on a special default unification) which under suitable conditions will appropriately extend world–paths which are too short.

Definition :
A world–path w is a prefix of a world–path w', denoted $w \preceq w'$, iff there exists a world–path z such that $w' = w + z$. (The symbol "+" denotes list concatenation.) ∎

Since in our applications, due to the syntactic structure of our plan generation problems and due to the assumption of unique interpretation of symbols in different worlds, all symbols in a literal are prefixed by the same world–path, we can restrict the definition of default unification to this case.

Definition :
$w_1 L_1$ and $w_2 L_2$ are **default–unifiable**, i.e. $\text{Dunif}(w_1 L_1, w_2 L_2)$
iff w.r.t.g. there is a prefix w of w_2, i.e. $w \preceq w_2$, such that $w_1 L_1$ and wL_2 are unifiable. A pair of complementary default–unifiable literals is called a **default connection**. (We get ordinary unification as a special case of default unification for $w = w_2$.) ∎

How default connections help to avoid the use of frame axioms can be seen again in our example.

Example :

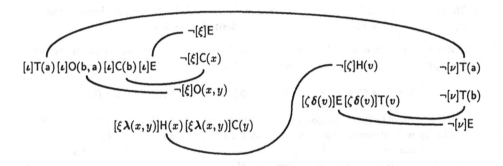

However, default connections cannot be allowed unrestrictedly; this would lead us back to a monotonic logic—all facts would survive all actions—and, in addition, would result in incorrect plans.

Since the antecedent of a rule incorporates the set of facts which will be false after the execution of the corresponding action, we should restrict default connections to literals which are not otherwise connected, whether by ordinary connections or by other default connections. But there are still problems which arise, if in a matrix there are two literals, say $w_1 L_1$ and $w_2 L_2$ which are both in the consequent of rules and a literal wL in the antecedent of a rule r, such that they default–unify simultaneously under the same substitution, i.e. there are subpaths $w_1' \preceq w$ and $w_2' \preceq w$ and a substitution σ such that $\sigma(L_1) = \sigma(L_2) = \sigma(L)$ and $\sigma(w_2 L_2) = \sigma(w_2' L)$ and $\sigma(w_1 L_1) = \sigma(w_1' L)$. If now for the application of rule r, for instance, $w_1 L_1$ is connected to the literal wL, but $w_2 L_2$ is not, then the latter one—being still unconnected—would further on be available for a default connection during the application of a rule after the application of r. Of course, the survival of $w_2 L_2$ would be precluded in case of reasoning more explicitly by frame axioms.

Let us think about the reasons for this kind of problem; how can it arise? First of all, nothing prevents us from deriving one and the same formula as often as we want, as well as from multiplying arbitrarily conjuncts and disjuncts in formulae. But anomalies of this kind can generally be avoided by imposing some discipline on the proof process—a discipline which is desirable anyhow for minimizing the size of proofs—in particular when handling the rather simple formulae of our planning problems.

Unfortunately, apart from these less problematic cases, we must also be in for the occurrence of multiple literal generation which is intrinsically due to the shape of certain rules, i.e to the way certain actions are represented. For instance, it might happen that a sequence of rules reproduces more or less the situation it set out from, however augmented by a new fact L. Such a sequence of rules could now be reapplied infinitely, whereby it will furnish new instances of L again and again. Applying now a rule which has L as a precondition, will only remove one copy of L, letting all the others survive. Although such effects may generally be precluded by exercising great circumspection in choosing the knowledge representation language and in specifying the rules, nevertheless we cannot evade having to be prepared for them.

Let us therefore impose some conditions on proofs performed with the modal logic, which will guarantee the correct use of default connections.

Definition :
For a ground and pure planning problem a **matrix–oriented situation description** is defined in the following way:

- The multiset of (modally prefixed) literals $[wL_1, \ldots, wL_n]$ reflecting the initial situation $\Diamond(F_1 \wedge \ldots \wedge F_n)$ in the matrix is a matrix–oriented situation description.

- Given the matrix–oriented situation description $[w_1L_1, \ldots, w_mL_m]$ and an already appropriately instantiated frame axiom (or rule)

$$\Box\Big(C_1 \wedge \ldots \wedge C_l \wedge A_1 \wedge \ldots \wedge A_g \longrightarrow \Diamond(C_1 \wedge \ldots \wedge C_l \wedge B_1 \wedge \ldots \wedge B_h)\Big)$$

which is applied to this situation such that the literals $C_1, \ldots C_l, A_1, \ldots, A_g$ are linked—maybe by default connections—w.r.t.g. to the literals $w_1L_1, \ldots, w_{l+g}L_{l+g}$, then the multiset $[w_{l+g+1}L_{l+g+1}, \ldots, w_mL_m] \cup [vC_1, \ldots, vC_l, vB_1, \ldots, vB_h]$, is the matrix–oriented description of a (new) situation. ∎

Intuitively a matrix–oriented situation description consists of all literals in consequent position of rules (and frame axioms) in the matrix, which are unconnected at a given arbitrary moment of a forward reasoning proof process. In contrast to the description of a situation—which could be defined analogously as a set of literals instead of a multiset—the matrix–oriented description takes into account the different instances of a fact that may emerge in a matrix.

Definition :
A compound instance corresponding to a ground and pure planning problem with default connections is called **u–normal** iff every matrix–oriented situation description $[w_1L_1, \ldots, w_mL_m]$ and each of its submultisets $[w'_1L'_1, \ldots, w'_sL'_s] \subset [w_1L_1, \ldots, w_mL_m]$, such that $L'_1 = \ldots = L'_s$ satisfies the following two conditions:

- At most one of the $w'_1L'_1, \ldots, w'_sL'_s$ may be involved in a default connection.

- If one of the $w'_1L'_1, \ldots, w'_sL'_s$ is involved in a default connection, then none of these literals must be involved in an ordinary connection. ∎

The definition captures the intuitively obvious idea, that a fact exists at most once in a particular situation, independently of how often it is mentioned. This is in accordance with (classical and modal) logic where $\mathcal{F} \leftrightarrow \mathcal{F} \wedge \mathcal{F}$. Our frame axioms, since being nothing but ordinary logic, cope well with this fact—they check an arbitrary number of occurrences of a literal—but default connections act less cautiously.

The concept of u–normality allows several ways for implementing it. Since derivations are generally u–normal—provided some discipline in derivation—we could develop proofs without bothering about u–normality at all and postpone a respective verification till after the proof has been completed. On the other hand, we could control u–normality immediately for predicates which we suspect to infringe. We could even take refuge to the frame axioms when dealing with such facts.

Theorem :
Every u–normal complementary matrix with default connections can be extended to a proof without default connections.

Proof idea:
Given a default connection form a rule r_p to a rule r_{p+n}, we can replace it by a default connection from rule r_{p+1} to r_{p+n}. (in case of $n = 2$ we get an ordinary connection.) Thus, we finally replace iteratively this default connection by $n-1$ ordinary connections. This can be done for all original default connections. ∎

The importance of this theorem is that, due to the possibility to get rid of default connections, our proofs are correct with respect to the standard semantics of modal logics.

4. LIMITATIONS OF THE PRIMITIVE MODAL PLANNING LOGIC

Though the primitive modal planning logic which we developed in section 2 is quite powerful, it suffers under extreme conditions from a limited flexibility in expressing which facts will become false during the application of an action. This is the dark side of the fusion of preconditions and destructive effects of an action, which was quite favourable for enabling the regular structure of the frame axioms and later the application of our default reasoning. Let us show by means of some examples, which problems may arise:

Example 1:
Imagine a blocks world with black and white blocks together with some rules which, in order to be applicable, require certain blocks to be black. Thus it may occur that we want a certain block to be black. Since this block may be white in the current situation, it is quite desirable to be provided with an action which paints a particular block black, if necessary. (It should go without saying that our robot is physically able to paint.)

Independently of the way our robot paints, we will get a rule which has the following skeleton: $\Box\Big(\ldots \longrightarrow \Diamond(\ldots \wedge \mathsf{black}(y) \wedge \ldots)\Big)$

The points at issue are the points in the antecedent: since blocks which are painted black may be assumed to be white before the action is carried out, we might expect to discover the literal $\mathsf{white}(y)$ in the rule's antecedent. Its presence there, however, has the disadvantage that we must know—it must be explicitly stated—that a block is white, if we want to paint it black. This contradicts our intuition which maintains that a block can be painted black independently of what we know about the colour it had before. On the other hand, if $\mathsf{white}(y)$ is not in the antecedent of the painting rule and we apply this rule to a block, say b, which is explicitly declared to be white—this means we have the literal $\mathsf{white}(b)$ in our matrix—then this fact would erroneously survive (by means of the frame axioms as well as it would remain accessible to default connections) and we would create a situation where both $\mathsf{black}(b)$ and $\mathsf{white}(b)$ are valid. ∎

Example 2:
Further problems arise if the extension of a predicate varies too arbitrarily in different situations. Let's again assume a blocks world. As long as blocks are piled up nicely one on top of another, we don't run into problems, but we are no more able to cope with a world where blocks can be placed on an arbitrary number of others. (Here world doesn't mean possible world in the sense of modal logic, but the space of descriptive possibilities allowed by the used knowledge representation language and the application domain we want to model.)

For instance, if our world allows the following two possibilities for how blocks can be piled up

In order to pick up block a in the first situation, the pick–up rule

$$\Box \forall x, y \left(C(x) \wedge O(x,y) \wedge E \longrightarrow \Diamond \big(H(x) \wedge C(y)\big)\right) \quad (P_1)$$

given with the example in the introduction would do.

But the application of this rule in the second case would result in a situation where block a is in the hand of the robot, but in the situation's representation a would still be on top of block b or block c, depending on whether $[y \leftarrow c]$ or $[y \leftarrow b]$ was applied. To prevent the generation of such physically inconsistent situations we might think of building a rule like

$$\Box \forall x, y \left(C(x) \wedge O(x,y) \wedge O(x,z) \wedge E \longrightarrow \Diamond \big(H(x) \wedge C(y) \wedge C(z)\big)\right) \quad (P_2)$$

which allows us to match both facts $O(x,y)$ and $O(x,z)$ and to create a situation in which the block a is in the robot's hand and the tops of both b and c are clear. However, the correct application of (P_2) is by no means guaranteed: It could be applied as well with the substitution $[y \leftarrow b, z \leftarrow b]$ which would make the literals $O(x,y)$ and $O(x,z)$ coincide, as well as the literals $C(y)$ and $C(z)$, thus virtually resulting in rule (P_1) and the problems encountered with it.

Repairing our rule again by requiring the two lower blocks to be different

$$\Box \forall x, y \left(C(x) \wedge O(x,y) \wedge O(x,z) \wedge y \neq z \wedge E \longrightarrow \Diamond \big(H(x) \wedge C(y) \wedge C(z)\big)\right) \quad (P_3)$$

we finally get a rule which does its job well in the second situation. Unfortunately, to cope with the first situation as well, we must have rule (P_1) additionally in our system. (The reader may restart reading shortly after the last figure ...) ∎

5. AN EXTENDED MODAL PLANNING LOGIC

Despite the relative exceptionality of the examples discussed in the preceding section, it is nevertheless interesting to look for an extension of our system which can handle them. To achieve the flexibility required from our rules in order to cope with these examples, we will define sets of hierarchically ordered formulae instead of just single rules. The idea is that a rule should have stable parts—the ones that correspond to antecedent and consequent of the rules in the old system—as well as further addenda by which the stable parts can be arbitrarily extended; thus enabling the rules to affect an arbitrary number of facts. More formally, we get the following definition of an extended modal planning logic: (The first two points remain the same.)

Definition :

- The **initial situation** given by a set of facts $F_1, \ldots, F_n$. Postulating its existence, we want as an axiom their conjunction to be possible :

$$\Diamond(F_1 \wedge \ldots \wedge F_n) \qquad (I)$$

- The **goal** given also by a set of facts, say $G_1, \ldots, G_k$, indicates a situation the existence of which we want to prove from the axioms, i.e. the possibility of their conjunction :

$$\Diamond(G_1 \wedge \ldots \wedge G_k) \qquad (G)$$

- A rule is specified by a nested list of literals $\big[PD, AS, [pd_1, as_1], \ldots, [pd_r, as_r]\big]$ where the $PD, AS, pd_1, as_1, \ldots, pd_r, as_r$ are sets of literals.

  In addition, we have a formation law which determines the formulae—which we will call rules as well—to be produced from such a rule specification. These formulae are of the form:

$$\Box\Big(PD \wedge pd'_1 \wedge \ldots \wedge pd'_s \longrightarrow \Diamond(AS \wedge as'_1 \wedge \ldots \wedge as'_s)\Big)$$

  Here the pairs $[pd'_i, as'_i]$ are copies of pairs $[pd_i, as_i]$, where those variables have been renamed which are not among the variables occurring in PD.

  Extending such a formula by a further pair $[pd'_{s+1}, as'_{s+1}]$ will be called **rule expansion**.

  As before we get the frame axioms as *regular* extensions of a rule. They shall assure now that each set of facts $C_1, \ldots, C_l$ which are independent from the literals in $PD, pd_1, \ldots, pd_r$ are also valid in the new situation.

$$\Box\Big(C_1 \wedge \ldots \wedge C_l \wedge PD \wedge pd'_1 \wedge \ldots \wedge pd'_s$$
$$\wedge \text{INDEP}(C_1, PD, pd_1, \ldots, pd_r) \wedge \ldots \wedge \text{INDEP}(C_l, PD, pd_1, \ldots, pd_r)$$
$$\longrightarrow \Diamond(C_1 \wedge \ldots \wedge C_l \wedge AS \wedge as'_1 \wedge \ldots \wedge as'_s)\Big)$$

  This extension of a rule will be called **frame axiom extension**.

  The set of literals $\{PD, pd_1, \ldots, pd_r\}$ will be called the **formal delete list**.

  The literals of PD and AS are called the **nucleus** or **stable part** of a rule. ∎

As before, in the case of a pure plan generation problem independence may be reduced to differentness, i.e. we replace $\text{INDEP}(C_i, \{A_1, \ldots, A_g\})$ by $C_i \not\equiv A_1 \wedge \ldots \wedge C_i \not\equiv A_g$ and specify $\equiv$ as unifiable. INDEP may then be implemented as being equivalent to failure in the respective attempts of unification. Moreover, the independence of the rule expansion and the frame axiom extension should be noted.

Let us come back to the examples of the preceding section and show how we can handle them with the methods just developed:

Examples :
To cope with the *painting example* we specify the rules and frame axioms by

$$[\{\ \}, \{\text{black}(y)\}, [\{\text{white}(y)\}, \{\ \}]]$$

from which we get the rule

$$\Box \forall y \left(\longrightarrow \Diamond\text{black}(y)\right)$$

The crucial fact is that we are not allowed to construct a frame axiom of the form:

$$\Box \forall y \left(\dots \wedge \mathsf{white}(y) \wedge \dots \longrightarrow \Diamond \left(\dots \wedge \mathsf{white}(y) \wedge \mathsf{black}(y) \right) \right)$$

Note that a pure rule expansion is superfluous in this case, because it will not allow us to produce new facts.

To adapt the pick–up rule to a world with *pyramids* we must specify it as $[\{E, C(x)\}, \{H(x)\}, [\{O(x,y)\}, \{C(y)\}]]$. At first we can build the rule

$$\Box \forall x \left(E \wedge C(x) \longrightarrow \Diamond H(x) \right) \qquad (P_1)$$

Applied to a block a this rule still says nothing about the blocks supporting block a; but we are no longer allowed to shift relations like $O(a,y)$ for any y. To find out which blocks will become clear after a has been picked up, we must experiment (iteratively) with expansions like

$$\Box \forall x,y \left(E \wedge C(x) \wedge O(x,y) \longrightarrow \Diamond(H(x) \wedge C(y)) \right)$$

and $\qquad \Box \forall x,y,z \left(E \wedge C(x) \wedge O(x,y) \wedge O(x,z) \longrightarrow \Diamond(H(x) \wedge C(y) \wedge C(z)) \right)$

and so on.

Note that the variable y which doesn't occur in the stable part of the rule has been renamed to z in the second copy of $O(x,y)$. ∎

As in the case of the primitive modal planning system we would like to avoid the use of frame axioms. To this end we will extend default non–reasoning to the new state of affairs. The concepts of default unification, u–normality and matrix–oriented situation description remain the same, but note that there may be discrepancies between matrix–oriented situation descriptions and the corresponding *real* situations, because there may still be unconnected literals in the matrix—e.g. a literal $\mathsf{white}(x)$ in the painting example—which *in reality* are no longer valid. But these literals do no harm, because no frame axiom will be able to shift them to more recent situations and—as we will see below—default connections with them will not be allowed.

The concept of *groundness* must be generalized as follows:

Definition :
A plan generation problem of the extended system is **ground** iff

- all literals of the initial situation are ground

- for every rule specified by $[PD, AS, [pd_1, as_1], \dots, [pd_r, as_r]]$ the variables occurring in AS are a subset of the variables in PD and for all pairs $[pd_i, as_i]$ $(1 \le i \le r)$ the variables occurring in as_i are a subset of the variables in pd_i. ∎

The decisive adaption is that default connections must be more restricted.

Definition :
A default unification between the two literals $w_1 L_1$ and $w_2 L_2$ —with a prefix $w \preceq w_2$, i.e. there is a path w' such that $w + w' = w_2$, such that $w_1 L_1$ and $w L_2$ are unifiable—is **admissible** iff L_2 doesn't unify with a literal in the formal delete list of a rule corresponding to a world–constant in w'. ∎

Theorem :
Every u–normal complementary matrix with admissible default connections can be extended to a proof without default connections.

Proof :
The proof is analogous to the proof in section 3: it is the admissibility condition which guarantees the formation of the required frame axioms. ∎

The proposed extension of the system of section 2 requires a relatively great computational expenditure in comparison to the primitive system. In particular, it is the admissibility constraint which puts a considerable burden of search on the default reasoning. Therefore it is interesting to note that the admissibility check can be restricted to predicates which occur in the non–stable parts of rules. Default connections with other literals can be made as unrestrictedly as before; just beware of infractions of u–normality. We will therefore be anxious to try but cautiously with the newly acquired possibilities:

- In cases like the painting problem we can stick to the primitive system if we keep the descriptions of the situations complete, e.g. the colour of each block must be stated in the initial situation and we must specify all rules in a way, such that no block may lose its colour.

- Cases like taking a block from the top of several others are more difficult, because their treatment by the primitive system would require another representation of facts, i.e. another knowledge representation language to be used.

CONCLUSION

The ideas presented in this paper emerged during the study of another proposal for logic based plan generation: so called linear proofs [BIB 86b]. While investigating their semantics, a translation into a modal logic—especially designed for this purpose—was envisaged and partly accomplished. This comparative exercise lead to the idea of taking ordinary modal logic and incorporating there some of the following principles being implicitly assumed in the linear proofs approach.

- Time is separated from the facts. This is in sharp contrast to systems like the situational calculus where a time parameter is attached to each literal. Linear proofs use special literals to keep track of time, while we use modal operators. Both techniques work on the language level of whole formulae and not on the lower level of literals.

- The problem of deleting facts is solved via a restriction of their use, i.e. deletion is not solved by features of the language, but by means of control. In our model system we combine both possibilities: with frame axioms on the language level and with default connections (which may only use unconnected literals) on the control level.

- The restriction of use being employed is imposing an upper bound of one on the connectability of literals. This criterion has been refined through the concept of u–normality and, moreover, has been restricted to default connections.

Let us briefly summarize what we consider to be the advantages over linear proofs:

- Linear proofs are more a syntactical mechanism, than a logic. Our system is undoubtedly a logical one, but possessing a syntactical trick to shortcut proofs. The application of this trick is not mandatory and due to the possibility of removing default connections we do not step outside of logic. (Default connections have some faint resemblance to factorization techniques and can therefore be seen in this tradition to facilitate proofs (see [BIB 86a] or [FRO 83]).)

- While exploring the semantics hidden behind linear proofs, the concept of u–normality turned out to be crucial for their translation into other logical formalisms, thus endowing them with precise semantics. In cases where u–normality is infringed very often during the application of default connections, we can go back to the frame axioms, whereas with linear proofs we are left without such a last resort.

REFERENCES

[BIB 86a] BIBEL, W.: Automated Theorem Proving, (second edition), Vieweg 1986.

[BIB 86b] BIBEL, W.: A Deductive Solution for Plan Generation, New Generation Computing, 4 (1986) 115–132.

[FRO 83] FRONHÖFER, B.: On Refinements of the Connection Method, COLLOQUIA MATHEMATICA SOCIETATIS JANOS BOLYAI 42, Algebra, Combinatorics and Logic in Computer Science, Györ, Hungary, 1983, pp. 391–401.

[FRO 87] FRONHÖFER, B.: Linearity and Plan Generation, New Generation Computing 5 (1987) 213–225.

[FRO 89] Fronhöfer, B.: Default Connections in a Modal Planning Framework, Technical Report FKI–108–89, Institut für Informatik, TU München.

[JAC 87] JACKSON, P.; REICHGELT, H.: A General Proof Method for First–Order Logic, IJCAI–87, 10th International Joint Conference on Artificial Intelligence, Milan, Italy, August 87 (J. McDermott, ed.) pp. 942–944.

[OHL 88] OHLBACH, H.-J.: A Resolution Calculus for Modal Logics, CADE–88, Argonne, Illinois, USA, May 1988 (E. Lusk, R. Overbeek, eds.) pp. 500–516.

[WAL 87] WALLEN, L.: Matrix Proof Methods for Modal Logics, IJCAI–87, 10th International Joint Conference on Artificial Intelligence, Milan, Italy, August 87 (J. McDermott, ed.) pp. 917–923.

Recursive Plans

G.R. Ghassem-Sani and S.W.D. Steel

COMPUTER SCIENCE DEPARTMENT
UNIVERSITY OF ESSEX
COLCHESTER, CO4 3SQ

ABSTRACT

It is generally agreed that a planner should be able to reason with uncertain and iterative behaviours because many actions in real world have such behaviours. Some of earlier non-linear planners have approached these issues, nevertheless, the way that they handle the problem has not been logically derived. We introduce a new type of non-linear plans, *Recursive Plans*, which can be used to solve a class of conditional and recursive problems. The idea, which has been implemented, is based on mathematical induction.

1. INTRODUCTION

A planner should be able to reason with uncertain and iterative behaviours because many actions in real world have such behaviours. Some of earlier non-linear planners have approached these issues, nevertheless, the way that they handle the problem has not been logically derived. For instance, in Warplan-C (Warren, 1976) the issue of uncertainty was tackled by planning all branches of a conditional action which led to a redundant tree-structured plan. NOAH (Sacerdoti, 1977), the first implemented non-linear planner, can model an iterative action as a single entity. Actions in SIPE (Wilkins, 1984) are allowed to loop over a list of objects. However, these planners work only where the number of objects on which the iteration is to be performed is known; whilst the most important application of iteration is where we are not certain about the number of iterations. Steel (1988) has also proposed a solution to the iteration issue which is analogous to the FOR constructs in structured programming languages and has been partially implemented (Ghassem-sani, 1988). The proposal works on the assumption that there is a constant function from numbers to objects. Another approach to iteration is plan nets (Drummond, 1986). Plan nets are more expressive than the conventional procedural nets, used by non-linear planners, because they permit representation of the loops. However, the problem is that it seems much more difficult to implement a planner to generate plan nets. Furthermore, termination of a plan net may not be provable. Manna and Waldinger's deductive synthesis method (Manna & Waldinger, 1980) is another approach to the issues of uncertainty and iteration. They have mostly used their method to synthesize programs rather than plans. Recently, however, they introduced a slightly different version of situational calculus (McCarthy, 1963), plan theory, and applied their method to planning (Manna & Waldinger, 1987). Their method is sound and general but fairly complicated. Note that we are particularly interested in control of the search process. We have chosen the framework of non-linear planning because it is well-understood and a relatively easily controllable process. Manna and Waldinger's deductive method is general but hard to control. Therefore, we are prepared to sacrifice the generality for the sake of controllability.

It is agreed that the rules of or-elimination and induction (in theorem proving) are related to conditionals and recursive statements (in program synthesis), respectively. Our aim has been to incorporate these rules in non-linear planning. Having preserved the principle of non-linear planning, we introduce a new strategy, *Recursive Non-linear Planning*, which can be used to solve a class of conditional and iterative problems. The main idea, which has been inspired by (Manna & Waldinger, 1987) on one hand and (Boyer & Moore, 1979) on the other hand, is based on mathematical induction. We have also implemented a planning system to generate recursive plans. The system is currently running on several different problems.

2. Boyer and Moore's Induction Principle

It seems that the Boyer and Moore's theorem prover (Boyer & Moore, 1979) is so far the most powerful system in which the induction principle has been extensively used. Using a slightly different notation, their definition of the induction principle is as follows:

Suppose that

    (a) P and Q are predicates;
    (b) < denotes a well-founded relation;
    (c) f is a function;
    (d) x is a variable;
    (e) $P(x) \rightarrow f(x) < x$ is a theorem.

Then in order to prove that $Q(x)$ is a theorem, it is sufficient to prove:

    (1) $\sim P(x) \rightarrow Q(x)$ (i.e. the base case) and;
    (2) $(P(x) \& Q(f(x))) \rightarrow Q(x)$ (i.e. the step case) are theorems,

in which $Q(f(x))$ is the so-called induction hypothesis. The above definition is sufficient for the simple cases in which there are only one base case and one step case. In general, however, it might be necessary to prove several base and step cases. We do not present their definition of general case here.

3. RECURSIVE NON-LINEAR PLANS

Similar to an ordinary non-linear plan, a recursive plan is a partially ordered set of nodes. Each node in a recursive plan is identified by a unique integer code. All nodes have also their own pre- and postconditions. Postconditions of the unique node *begin* (code 1) represents the initial state and preconditions of the unique node *end* (code 2) represents the goal state. The so-called ranges, which are 3-ary tuples <Producer, User, Condition> represented by '===...===', are to protect certain conditions at certain parts of plans. Actions are 4-ary tuples of form <Name, Preconds, Effects, Delete-list>. Although a recursive plan and an ordinary non-linear plan are very similar, there are three new type of nodes that may appear only in a recursive plan. These nodes are called CASE, PROC, and CALL which are analogous to the CASE, PROCEDURE, and CALL statements in programming languages.

3.1. CASE Nodes

Each CASE node in a recursive plan has a number of internal plan. Internal plans of a CASE node have different initial states, but all have the same goal state. Preconditions of node *begin* in internal plans act as labels. During the execution depending on the state of the world at the time of choosing an internal plan, any internal plan whose label is true in the world can be chosen to be executed.

The following figure shows a typical CASE node.

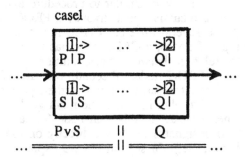

casel

Note that we assume all labels in CASE nodes are testable in the sense considered in the problem of the 'monkey, bomb, and banana' of (Manna & Waldinger, 1987).

From outside, a CASE node is like an ordinary node with its own pre- and postconditions. The disjunction of labels of the internal plans form preconditions of CASE nodes; and the postcondition of a CASE node is equal to the goal states of its internal plans. Each internal plan is itself a recursive plan, which means it might comprise a number of CASE nodes. However, the innermost internal plans comprise no CASE node.

In general, there are two situations where we add a CASE node to a recursive plan. First if there is an unsupported precondition P and there is either a node in the plan or an action in the repertoire with postconditions including a disjunctive sentence of form '... v P v ...', then a CASE node is generated to support P. The second situation where a CASE node is generated corresponds to the case analysis of an inductive proof and has been adopted from Boyer and Moore (1979) who say:

"To apply the principle of induction to a conjecture, we must invent a case analysis, together with some substitution, a variable n-tuple, a measure, and a well-founded relation. We must prove the conjecture under each of the cases."

By analogy and in non-linear terms we claim that to apply the principle of induction to a goal we should generate a CASE node whose internal plans correspond to the appropriate case analysis. How one could achieve a goal by a CASE node, is discussed in section (4).

Finally, after a CASE node is generated, it will be added to the action repertoire (with a similar format to that of ordinary actions) as a new action, which could be later used to create CALL nodes.

3.2. PROC Nodes

PROC nodes in recursive plans are analogous to a special case of sub-procedures in programming languages. A PROC node, here, is essentially a CASE node. To be more precise, if a generated CASE node is invoked by a CALL node (discussed next), it will be tactically renamed into a PROC node. There are two reasons behind renaming some of CASE nodes into PROC nodes. First to keep the analogy between recursive plans and imperative programs as much as possible; and, more importantly, to prepare recursive plans for the task of detecting and, if necessary, resolving conflicts. Since PROC nodes (together with CALL nodes) form recursion, detecting conflicts involving internal plans of a PROC node is both different from and more difficult than for a CASE node. Therefore, from now on, we refer to any CASE node which is invoked by a CALL node as a PROC node.

3.3. CALL Nodes

A CALL node in our system is very similar to procedure invocation in imperative languages. A CALL node in a recursive plan invokes a PROC node. Although it is not very likely, there might be several different CALL nodes calling the same PROC node. Similarly to other type of nodes, a CALL node has its own pre- and postconditions. There is always a relation between postconditions of a CALL node and postconditions of the invoked PROC node. Preconditions of a CALL node and the invoked PROC node have exactly the same relation as their postconditions have. The following figure shows a recursive plan in which the main goal is to make the base of a tower of blocks (i.e. 'a' here) clear. In this plan node 5 is a CALL, 4 an ordinary, and 3 a PROC node. (hat(a) designates the block directly on top of a, hat(hat(a)) the block directly on top of hat(a), etc.) In section (4) we explain how such a recursive plan is generated.

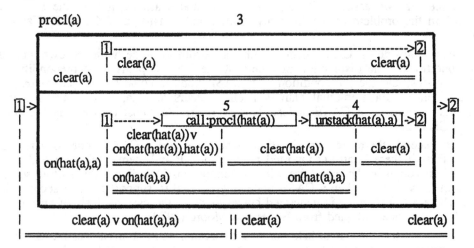

3.4. Relation between Recursive Plans and Induction Principle

It was earlier said that recursive plans are based on the Boyer and Moore's induction principle. The following figure shows their induction principle in contrast with a general form of a simple recursive plan.

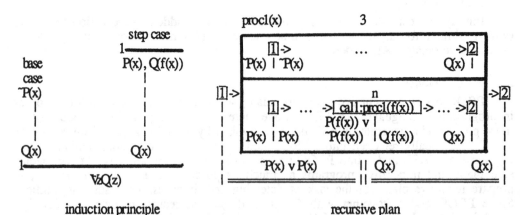

induction principle   recursive plan

The first internal plan of *proc1* corresponds to the base case of the induction principle and the second internal plan to its step case.

4. PLANNING PROCESS

4.1. Overview

Before explaining the planning process, let us call our system RNP (Recursive Non-linear Planner). Conventional operations, by which non-linear planners achieve a subgoal in order to modify an incomplete plan, are linking to an old node, and adding a new node to the plan. Apart from conventional operations, RNP can improve an incomplete plan by two new operations: creating a CALL node, and generating a CASE node. (Note that PROC nodes are produced by renaming those CASE nodes which are invoked by CALL nodes. Therefore, RNP does not have a separate operation to generate PROC nodes). RNP applies its modification operations to an incomplete plan in the following order:

(1): linking to an old node,
(2): creating a CALL node,
(3): adding a new (ordinary) node,
(4): generating a CASE node.

Why have we chosen the above order? The last three of the above operations add a new node to an incomplete plan. Each time that a new node is added to a plan, the node's preconditions will be appended to the list of unsupported preconditions which must be achieved. The first operation (i.e. linking to an old node) should have a higher priority than that of the other three, because it appends nothing to the list of unsupported preconditions. Among the last three operations, generating a CASE node is more time consuming and complicated than the others; because, unlike the others, it involves generating a number of internal plans. Thus, generating a CASE node should have the least priority of these operations. Finally, creating a CALL node should be tried before adding a new simple node, because otherwise the planner is likely to be trapped in a loop. Consider, for instance, the following action:

$$\boxed{A}$$
$$P(f(X)) \mid P(X)$$
$$\mid$$

Suppose that the planner is to achieve the subgoal $P(a)$. It improves the plan by action A and then $P(f(a))$ will be its new subgoal. If, at that stage, the planner applied the operation (3) before (2), it would choose action A again and then $P(f(f(a)))$ would be the next new subgoal. Had the planning process continued this way, the planner would have never tried to create a CALL node; whilst, as we later see, the planner should in fact try to achieve $P(f(a))$ by a CALL node.

The search method used by RNP is iterative deepening, so search will not fall into the infinite branches of repeated use of any of these operations. There is of course an issue of correctness and completeness. We believe but have not shown that the planner is correct; it is almost certainly not complete.

4.2. Generating CASE Nodes

Generating a CASE node is the last resort by which RNP tries to improves an incomplete plan. However, we explain it first for the sake of simplicity and providing some information for the subsequent sub-sections. We do not explain conventional operations (1) and (3) above. Consider the following partial plan:

```
 1-->   ...   -->6        5-->4-->3-->2
 |               |PvS     P| Q | R | G |
 |               |        |==|==|==|==|
```

Suppose that the planner is trying to achieve the subgoal P of node 5. Let us call node 5, the user. If RNP fails to achieve P by either conventional operations (1 and 3 above) or by adding a CALL node (discussed later), it will try to achieve P by generating a CASE node. In order to generate a CASE node, RNP searches for a node in the plan (or an action in the repertoire) with postconditions including a disjunctive sentence of the form '... v P v ...'. Let us call such a node the producer. If RNP fails to find such a producer, it will add the sentence '~P v P' (equivalent to truth) to the postconditions of node *begin* (code 1) and regard node *begin* as the producer. RNP then adds a CASE node to the plan to link the producer (eg. node 6) and the user (eg. node 5). The following figure shows the above partial plan after adding a CASE node.

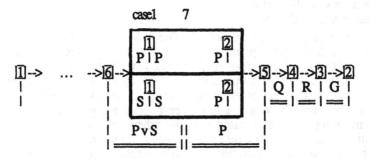

Now RNP has to generate the internal plans of the CASE node. Note that generating the first internal plan of the above CASE node is trivial. If RNP fails to generate any of these internal plans, the CASE node will be replaced by backtracking by another one as shown in the following figure. The new CASE node differs from the previous one mainly in the goal states of its internal plans.

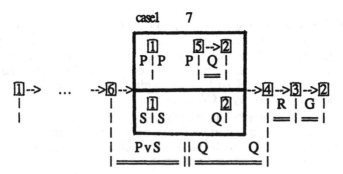

Backtracking may continue and each time a new CASE node, of which mostly the goal states of the internal plans change, would be tried, until finally RNP succeeds in generating all the internal plans of a CASE node. How does RNP choose the goal states of the internal plans in each try? Consider the above partial plan before adding *case1*, and suppose again that RNP is trying to achieve the subgoal P. RNP first finds all paths from node 5 to the node *end* (code 2). We use the PROLOG (Bratko, 1987) list notation, '[...]', to show a path. In this example there is only one such a path, [5, 4, 3, 2] (Members of a path are integer codes of nodes). In each try, RNP chooses one node of this path. Let us call this node the user. The preconditions of the user in each try form the goal states of the internal plans. Although in this example there is only one path between node 5 and node 2, in general there might exist several such paths. After all members of a path have been tried as the user, if backtracking continues, RNP will nominate the first member of another path as the new user.

Those nodes that precede the user in the path will be removed from the main plan. For example, if node 5 is chosen to be the user, nothing will be removed from the main plan because nothing precede node 5 in the path; but if, for instance after backtracking, node 4 is chosen to be the user, node 5 will be removed from the main plan. The intuition behind removing this part of the main plan is that this part will be included in one of the internal plans of the CASE node.

4.3. Creating CALL Nodes

4.3.1. Similar Subgoals

In order to create a CALL node, one needs to be able to recognise the appropriate time to do so. A similarity between a subgoal and a top level goal indicates the possibility of achieving the subgoal by recursion. Thus the problem is how to recognise the similarity between a subgoal and a top level goal. In general, a subgoal of form $Q(f(x))$ and a goal of form $Q(x)$, where x is a variable tuple, are similar; but how could one detect such similarity? It is clear that the similarity here does not mean being unifiable by the first order unification algorithm (Robinson, 1965). However, one can identify the similarity between such terms using typed-lambda unification algorithm (Huet, 1974). For this purpose we try to solve the following equation, in which '?...' indicates a variable and '==' means lambda unifiable:

$$\text{top level goal} == ?Q(?x), \text{ and subgoal} == ?Q(?f(?x)) \tag{1}$$

The above equation is solved by finding substitutions S1 and [?f:= ...] such that:

$$\text{top level goal} = ?Q(?x)S1, \text{ and subgoal} = (?Q(?f(?x))S1)[?f:= ...] \tag{2}$$

Having found such substitutions, one can conclude that the subgoal is similar to the top level goal. In the tower-clearing recursive plan shown in section 3.3, for instance, the subgoal clear(hat(a)) of node 4 (inside *proc1*) and the top level goal clear(a) of node 2 (outside *proc1*) are similar; because if we solve the equation (1) for these two goals, we will get the substitutions [?x:=a, ?Q:=clear] and [?f:=λ?z.hat(?z)] such that:

$$\text{clear(a)} = ?Q(?x)[?x:=a, ?Q:=clear], \text{ and}$$
$$\text{clear(hat(a))} = (?Q(?f(?x))[?x:=a, ?Q:=clear])[?f:=λ?z.hat(?z)]$$

Definition 1:

A subgoal SG is similar to a top level goal TG if and only if there exist S1 and F such that: TG = $?Q(?x)S1$, and SG = $(?Q(?f(?x))S1)[?f:= F]$ in which S1 is a substitution for the variables ?x and ?Q.

Although in general typed-lambda unification algorithm is expensive, the actual cost of using it in the cases encountered does not seem great; it might, however, be later proved that the full power of the algorithm is not necessary.

4.3.2. Termination Condition

The similarity between a subgoal and a top level goal, though necessary, is not sufficient for RNP to create a CALL node. Let us call this other precondition, which guarantees that recursive plans terminate, the termination condition. The condition corresponds to the precondition (e) of the induction principle explained in section 2.

For a subgoal $Q(f(x))$ similar to a goal $Q(x)$, the condition has the form of $P(x) \to f(x) < x$, in which P is a predicate, and < a well-founded relation. Roughly speaking, the termination condition ensures that the subgoal is a reduced (or simpler) form of the top level goal. Satisfiability of the termination condition is determined by looking up a table which is part of RNP's knowledge base. The table comprise, for instance, the following statements:

$$\tilde{} clear\_block(?x) \to hat(?x) < ?x,$$
$$\tilde{} empty\_list(?x) \to tail(?x) < ?x.$$

Definition 2:

A subgoal $Q(f(x))$ is a reduced form of a top level goal $Q(x)$ if and only if there exist a predicate P and a well-founded relation < such that:
$P(x) \to f(x) < x$.

4.3.3. Case Analysis

After a subgoal $Q(f(x))$ has been proved to be a reduced form of a top level goal $Q(x)$, RNP will try to achieve the subgoal by creating a CALL node invoking a suitable PROC node. But what is a suitable PROC node? A PROC node is suitable to be invoked by a CALL node to achieve $Q(f(x))$, if the PROC node produces $Q(x)$ and its internal plans cover the base and step cases of the corresponding inductive proof. For instance, the following figure shows the general form of a suitable PROC node in the simplest case, where the proof has only one base and one step case.

procl(x)

	base case	
[1] ~P(x) I ~P(x)		[2] Q(x) I
[1] P(x) I P(x)	step case	[2] Q(x) I

~P(x) v P(x) II Q(x)

Therefore, if there is a suitable PROC node such as *procl(x)* above, a CALL node *call:procl(f(x))* of the following form will be added to the developing plan, to achieve the subgoal $Q(f(x))$.

call:procl(f(x))
~P(f(x)) v P(f(x)) I Q(f(x))
I

But what if there is not such a PROC node? Having failed to find a suitable PROC node, RNP will try to generate one. Consider, for instance, the following partial plan.

[c] ->...->[b]-->[a]->...
Q(f(x)) I   I Q(x) I
       I   I === I

In situations such as the above partial plan, after failing to find a suitable PROC node, RNP would first try to generate a PROC node (i.e. generating and renaming a CASE node) to produce $Q(x)$, and then create a CALL node invoking the PROC node to achieve $Q(f(x))$. Next figure shows the above partial plan after generating a PROC node.

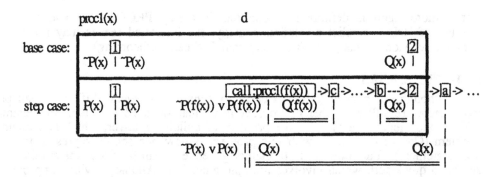

Note that some part of the original partial plan is now included in the PROC node. In order to complete the process of generating *proc1(x)*, RNP has to generate an internal plan for the base-case branch, and complete the step-case branch. Achieving subgoals '~P(x) v P(x)' and '~P(f(x)) v P(f(x))', which are equivalent to truth, is trivial.

4.4. Detecting & Resolving Conflicts

One of important tasks of a non-linear planner is the task of detecting and, if necessary, resolving conflicts. Apart from conflicts involving only ordinary nodes, in a recursive plan, we may also face conflicts involving CASE, PROC, or CALL nodes. RNP Detects conflicts involving CASE and PROC nodes by performing the following stages:

(1) replacing all CASE (and PROC) nodes by one of their internal plans, which transforms a recursive plan into a CASE-PROC-free non-linear plan (i.e. a plan without any CASE or PROC node),

(2) detecting conflicts of the CASE-PROC-free plan as an ordinary non-linear plan.

RNP then repeats this process for all combinations of internal plans of CASE (and PROC) nodes.

Although a CASE-PROC-free plan is treated like an ordinary non-linear plan, some of its nodes which originally belong to a PROC node (eg. CALL nodes) need a special conflict detection strategy. The fact that PROC nodes might be executed several times implies that there might exist a conflict involving only certain cycles of executing the PROC node. In general, a recursive plan is independent of the number of operands on which the plan may be executed. For instance, the tower-clearing plan, shown in section 3.3, can be used to clear the base of any tower consisting of any number of blocks. This makes the task of detecting conflicts involving PROC nodes difficult, because during the planning process it is not known how many times a PROC node might be executed. Nevertheless, we can predict the possibility of some conflicts (occurring in the execution time) during the planning process; because although one cannot forecast how many times a PROC node would be called, it is known that in each call all ranges inside the PROC node are a reduced form of that of the previous call (according to some well-founded relation and toward a base element). Now if there is a node (outside a PROC node) denying a condition which is a reduced form of a range inside the PROC node, there is the possibility of a conflict occurring in execution of the PROC node. For instance, if we assume there is a node N outside *proc1(a)* of the tower-clearing plan with the postcondition ~clear(hat(hat(a))), there would be such a possible conflict between range <5, 4, clear(hat(a))> (in the second internal plan of *proc1*) and node N, because node N denies clear(hat(hat(a))) which is a reduced form of clear(hat(a)).

For a more rigorous definition of conflicts involving PROC nodes and a detailed account of RNP's conflict resolution strategy, the interested reader may refer to the complete version of this paper (Ghassem-sani & Steel, forthcoming).

5. DEFICIENCIES

Although our planner (RNP) is currently running on several different small problems, there are still a number of improvements that we need to make. For example, RNP cannot generate a plan for the problem of building a tower, which is a recursive problem (One of difficulties with this problem is how one should represent the main goal statement). Furthermore, RNP cannot generate a plan for problems similar to the so-called quick-sort, which involves multiple recursion. Another obvious improvement is that to be able to generate recursive plans for inductive proofs involving more than only one base and one step cases. The difficulty, here, is to determine the appropriate initial states of internal plans corresponding to the base and step cases.

6. CONCLUSION

There are many actions in real world which have conditional and/or iterative behaviour. It is essential for a planning system to be able to model such actions. Contemporary non-linear planners, however, do not have such an ability. We have introduced and implemented a new strategy, *Recursive Non-linear Planning*, which enables a non-linear planner to handle a class of conditional and recursive problems. The process of generating these plans, which comprise a few new modification rule besides conventional rules used in ordinary non-linear planning, is based on mathematical induction.

REFERENCES

Boyer, R. S. and Moore, J. S. (1979)

ACM monograph series, A Computational Logic, Academic Press, INC. London

Bratko, I. (1987)

Prolog Programming for Artificial Intelligence, Academic Press, INC. London

Drummond, M. (1986)

A representation of action and belief for automatic planning systems, in: (Georgeff, M. and Lansky, A.), Morgan Kauffman

Ghassem-Sani, G. R. (1988)

Iterative actions in non-linear planners, M.Sc. Thesis, Department of Computer Science, University of Essex

Ghassem-Sani, G. R. and Steel, S. W. D. (forthcoming)

Recursive Plans, Internal Report, University of Essex

Huet, G. P. (1974)

A unification algorithm for typed lambda-calculus, note de travial A 055, Institute de Recherche d'Informatique et d'Automatique

Manna, Z. and Waldinger, R. (1980)

A deductive approach to programme synthesis, ACM Transactions on Programming Languages and Systems, 2(1), PP. 90-121

Manna, Z. and Waldinger, R. (1987)

How to clear a block: A Theory of plans, Journal of Automated Reasoning, Vol. 3, PP. 343-377

McCarthy J. (1963)

Situations, actions, and causal laws, Technical report, Stanford university, Stanford, Calf.

Robinson, J. A. (1965)

A machine oriented logic based on the resolution principle, J. ACM 12, No 1, PP. 23-41

Sacerdoti, E. D. (1977)

A Structure for Plans and Behaviour, American Elsevier North-Holland, New York

Steel, S. W. D. (1988)

An iterative construct for non-linear precedence planners, Proc. Seventh Biennial Conference of the Canadian Society for the Computational Study of Intelligence, PP. 227-233

Warren, D. H. D. (1976)

Generating Conditional Plans and Programmes, In Proceedings of the AISB summer conference, PP. 344-354

Wilkins, D. E. (1984)

Domain-independent Planning: Representation and Plan Generation, Artificial Intelligence 22(3), PP. 269-301

A Language for Representing Planning Problems

R. Göbel, R. Rodosek

Deutsche Forschungsanstalt für Luft- und Raumfahrt
Hauptabteilung Angewandte Datentechnik
D–8031 Oberpfaffenhofen

Abstract

In this paper we introduce a language for representing planning problems, planning decisions and plans in one formalism. This single representation supports the recognition and the analysis of dependencies between planning decisions and goals. The recognition and analysis of dependencies between decisions and goals is a central task for advanced planning procedures. A good support of this task directly improves the efficiency of the procedure and improves the quality of the generated plan.

1. Introduction

In this paper we introduce a new language for representing a big subclass of scheduling problems from the area of production planning. With this language one can represent planning problems, planning decisions and plans in one single formalism. This feature is essential for advanced planning procedures as we will see in section 4.

The type of scheduling problems that we will consider are job shop scheduling problems. For this class of problems one has to generate a production plan from a set of orders for a given production environment. Every of these orders specifies a product, a due date for the product and a priority for the order. For all products one or more production plans are given. A production plan has a set of production steps and a temporal order on these steps. A single production step may require one or more resources. Also there may be alternatives for the set of required resources. For every set of resources the duration of the production step has to be given.

We will start this paper with a description of the production environment for which the plans have to be generated (section 2). Then we will discuss several methods for generating plans (section 3) and describe the requirements for the method we will use. The language itself will be described in section 4. Finally we will discuss the language and give an overview on future work (section 5).

2. The German Remote Sensing Data Center

The German Remote Sensing Data Center (Deutsches Fernerkundungsdatenzentrum – DFD) is one of the german space centers located at the German Aerospace Research

Establishment in Oberpfaffenhofen. The DFD builds and runs on board and ground data segments for space applications. These segments are applied for collecting, transmitting and processing of satellite payload data.

One of the major tasks of the DFD is to process incoming satellite data and generate several products from the raw data. This processing requires usually several steps on several computers, therefore a production management is necessary. For this task the DFD currently develops a Facility Management System [DLR 1989], which will be available at the beginning of 1991.

The input of this Facility Management System (FMS) includes:

- orders which specify a product, a due date and a priority
- a sequence of productions steps for every product and a temporal order on these productions steps
- one or more sets of required resources for every step
- the available configuration (computers , peripherals, . . .)
- the status of every resource

From these and other inputs, the FMS has to generate a production plan and control the execution of the plan. A production plan may contain more than 1000 production steps which have to be assigned to more than 100 resources (computers and peripherals). A plan of this size has to be generated in less than 10 minutes, because a difference between the production status and the plan may require a replanning during the production process.

3. Methods for Generating Production Plans

In this section we will give an overview on several planning procedures. We will discuss their advantages and problems with respect to our application. Then we choose the best suited method and discuss its requirements.

We will start this section with a well known method for generating plans which comes from the area of Operations Research (subsection 3.1). Then we will describe a familiar AI approach for solving planning problems with search trees (subsection 3.2). Finally we discuss a rather new method where an initial plan is improved in several steps by modifying small parts of the plan (subsection 3.3) and discuss the requirements for this method (subsection 3.4).

3-1. Planning without Backtrack

A well known method for generating plans comes from the area of Operations Research. This method is already available in several products like KEE [KEE 1990], MARS [Kellner 1990] and TINA [Dornier 1990]. Also it has been successfully applied to several planning problems.

In a simple production environment where production steps have to be assigned to single resources and the only requirement is a partial ordering on the production steps, the planning procedure for this method works as follows:

1. Identify the set of all basic production steps: STEPS.
2. Choose a production step from STEPS which has no predecessors in STEPS. Remove it from the set STEPS.
3. Find all possible start times on every resource for the current step.
4. Choose a resource and a start time and assign it to the current step. Assign a finish time to the current step, which has been derived from the start time and the duration of the step on the chosen resource.
5. If the set STEPS is empty, then a plan has been generated, otherwise continue with step 1.

The structure of the generated plan is strongly dependent on the choice of the next production step (planning step 2), on the choice of the resource and the start time on it (planning step 4). Here one can apply several heuristics as for example chosing production steps with the highest priority or due date and chosing the resource with the earliest availability.

The advantage of this approach is that every production step is only considered once. Therefore the planning procedure is rather fast, the procedure has usually a linear time complexity.

Another major advantage of this method is that one can easily extend it. For the FMS for example, this method has been extended for handling production steps requiring more than one resource, resources with capacities, tools which are used up and some other features.

Unfortunately there are two serious problems which restrict the application of this method:

1. The generated plan does not always satisfy all specified requirements.
2. The procedure generates poor plans (use of resources, differences between due dates and creation times of a product, . . .).

These problems occur because one may recognize during the planning process that an earlier decision was wrong. Then it is not possible to go back to this decision and choose a different alternative.

3-2. Planning with Search Trees

The problems of the previous method can be avoided, if one considers every alternative for all decisions. The simple planning problem of subsection 3–1. requires choices for the following decisions:

1. Choose a resource for every production step

2. Choose a start time for the production step on its resource

For this approach one usually applies a search tree. Here every node of the search tree represents a decision and every path from a parent node to its child nodes represents an alternative for the decision. A path from the root to a leaf of the tree specifies a plan because an alternative for every decision has been chosen.

Usually the size of a search tree grows exponentially with its depth (number of decisions). Therefore a complete search tree can only be generated for very small problems. For bigger problems one has to avoid to consider every node of the search tree. Beneath others, the following methods to reduce the number of nodes (search space) are possible:

1. Use an efficient search procedure with a heuristic evaluation function for guiding the search (see for example: [Kanal, Kumar 1988]).

2. Find nodes where 'wrong' alternatives have been chosen and choose a different alternative for this decision (intelligent backtracking).

3. Reduce the number of possible alternatives by analyzing the problem and all alternatives which have been chosen for previous decisions.

Usually one combines all three methods for reducing the search space (see for example: [Fox 1990], [Fox, Sadeh, Baykan 1989]). But even with these methods the search tree grows exponentially with the size of a problem. The reason is that scheduling problems are in general NP-Hard. This means that one cannot hope for a method which generates an optimal or even a correct plan in polynomial time, even though it may exist.

3-3. Optimizing Plans

For a certain type of planning problems the methods from subsection 3–1. and 3–2. cannot be applied. Problems of this class are not small enough to be solved by a search tree method and the quality of the plans from a linear method does not meet the requirements. The planning problems from FMS seem to belong to this type:

1. The number of production steps and resources are high and it may increase in future.

2. The resources have to be used effectively and most of the due dates have to be satisfied.

The first requirement excludes a search tree method especially when the number of production steps and resources will be increased. The second requirement is not satisfied by a linear algorithm.

This type of scheduling problem may be solved by a plan optimization method. For this method one generates a plan with a fast algorithm and then tries to improve this plan:

1. Generate a first plan by choosing an alternative for every decision (for example with a linear method).

2. Find a requirement (for example a due date) which is not yet satisfied. Try to modify the plan such that the new plan satisfies this requirement. This new plan may not violate a requirement which has been satisfied by the old plan.

3. Continue with step 2 until no more improvements can be found.

The quality of the plan and the speed of the method depend strongly on the algorithm which one applies in step 2. A complete method for finding an improvement of the plan, if it exists, also has an exponential time complexity. On the other hand one can apply incomplete but fast methods which do not find all but only some improvements. Then this method may still have a polynomial time complexity but it generates far better plans than the linear method.

3-4. Requirements for Plan Optimization Techniques

A plan optimization procedure has to be able to analyze and modify plans. Therefore the input for the procedure has to be a plan in some readable form. Usually a plan is represented as a list of production step, where a set of resources and a start and finish time are assigned to every step. In this case the optimization procedure should modify the assignment and choose new resources, new start and new finish times for some steps.

A modification of this type of plan without additional knowledge is not possible, because new assignments are only allowed if they satisfy the problem description. But also the plan together with the problem description is not sufficient for an efficient plan optimization procedure. The problem is, that the reason for the assignments are not clear.

See for example the reason for a start time of a production step. Assume that a planning procedure chooses the earliest possible start time of a production step. Then for the earliest possible start time at least two different reasons may exist:

1. The production step is part of a sequence of production steps for processing an order. The finish time of a production step, which has to be finished before the current production step may start, is the start time of the current step.

2. The start time of the production step is the earliest time when its resource is available. In this case a different production step should run on the resource before the current step may start (choice of the planning procedure).

Assume now, that the plan optimization procedure wants to reduce the start time of the production step. For the first case the start time of the current step is restricted by a different step, which has to be finished before the current step. Therefore the procedure has to decrease the finish time of the previous step. For the second case it may also try to change the order of production steps on the required resource.

This example shows that the input for the plan optimization procedure has to be the plan, the problem specification and the reasons for all assignments of resources and times to all production steps. The reasons for the assignment are given either by the problem specification (case 1 of example) or by decisions of the planning procedure (case 2). Therefore the plan optimization procedure requires the following input:

- The plan
- A description of the problem
- The set of all planning decisions

This information should be available in one single language in order to simplify the major tasks of a plan optimization procedure:

- Analysis of dependencies between assignments, the problem description and the planning decisions
- Finding possible alternatives for an assignment
- Modify the plan by modifying planning decisions and assignments

4. Language Description

In this section we will introduce a single language for representing planning problems, planning decisions and plans. We will start the section with an informal introduction into the language (subsection 4-1.). The we will apply the language to a simple example and show how it can be applied to represent a problem (subsection 4-2.). Finally we show how a planning procedure and a plan optimization procedure may use this language (subsection 4-3.). A formal definition of the language can be found in [Göbel, Rodosek 1990].

4-1. An Informal Introduction

A specification of a planning problem in our language consists of the following constructs:

- Time intervals for specifying things like orders, production steps and availabilities of resources
- Numerical constraints for specifying the durations, the start and the finish times of time intervals
- Labels for specifying the priorities of time intervals
- Operators for specifying relationships between time intervals
- Definition of a subset of time intervals, which are specified as top intervals (usually all orders)

The time intervals will be represented as strings. These strings will be used as a reference for numerical constraints, for the labels and for the operators.

Every numerical constraint on a time interval a is specified by one of the following formulas:

- Latest start time of interval a is x: $START(a) \leq x$
- Earliest start time of interval a is x: $START(a) \geq x$
- Maximal duration of interval a is x: $DURATION(a) \leq x$
- Minimal duration of interval a is x: $DURATION(a) \geq x$
- Latest finish time of interval a is x: $END(a) \leq x$
- Earliest finish time of interval a is x: $END(a) \geq x$

For this language we will distinguish between soft and hard constraints. A hard constraint has to be satisfied, but soft constraints may be violated (as few as possible). The priority of an interval is given by a positive integer. The priority of an interval specifies the importance of its soft constraints. It is more important to satisfy the soft constraints of a time interval with a high priority than to satisfy the soft constraints of an interval with lower priority.

The relationships between the time intervals can be specified by the following operators:

- With the operator **before** ($<$) one can specify orders on time intervals representing for example production steps. An interval a is before an interval b, if the finish time of interval a is less or equal than the start time of interval b.

$a < b$:   [a]   [b]

- With the operator **equivalent** ($=$) one can specify, that two intervals a and b have the same start and finish times.

$a = b$:   [a]
           [b]

- With the operator **includes** ($\subset$) one can specify, that an interval contains a second interval. This of interest for orders which include production steps, or production steps which include substeps. An interval a includes an interval b if the start time of the interval a has to be greater or equal than the start time of the interval b. Further more, the finish time of the interval a has to be less or equal than the finish time of interval b.

$a \subset b$:   [b [a]]

- With the operator **no overlapping** (NOV) one can specify for example, that production steps on one machine may not overlap. This means, that for every two intervals b, c from a set A, either b is before c or c is before b.

$NOV(a_1,...,a_n)$:   [a_{i_1}]   ...   [a_{i_n}]

- With the operator OR one specifies alternatives for one time interval by a set of other time intervals A. Then the interval a is equivalent to one interval b from the set A. This is of interest, for example, when one has a production step for which alternatives for the set of resources exist. Note, that only one interval b from the set of alternatives will occur in a final plan.

$$OR(a, \{a_1, ..., a_n\}): \quad \boxed{a_1} \quad \cdots \quad \boxed{a_i} \quad \cdots \quad \boxed{a_n}$$
$$\boxed{a}$$

Note, that the binary relations before, equivalent and includes are closely related to some of Allen's relations ([Allen 1983]):

- Our relation before combines Allen's relations before and meets.
- Our relation equivalent is the same relation as Allen's equal relation.
- Our relation includes combines Allen's relations during, starts and finishes.

We specify the time intervals, which have to be in the final plan, by choosing a set of top intervals (usually the set of orders). These time intervals and all time intervals, which are included in a top interval either by the **equivalent** or the **include** operator, have to be in the plan.

Time interval, which occur not in a plan, should be member of a time interval of an OR relation, or should be included in an interval from an OR relation.

4-2. An Example

Now we will show how to represent planning problems with this language, by applying it to a simple planning problem. For this planning problem we consider three orders (order 1, order 2, order 3), specifying three products which have to be produced. The product for order 1 requires two production steps (step 1.1, step 1.2), the product for order 2 requires three production steps (step 2.1, step 2.2, step 2.3) and the product for order 3 again requires two production steps (step 3.1, step 3.2). These production steps can be carried out on three different machines (machine A, machine B, machine C). Some of these production steps require a fixed resource (step 1.2 on A, step 2.2 on B, step 3.1 on C, step 3.2 on C), where others may run on different machines (step 1.1 on A or B, step 2.1 on A or B, step 2.3 on C or B).

We will start to describe this planning problem by specifying a time interval for every order, every production step and every possible assignment of a machine to a production step. The time interval for an order is a representation for the real time interval where the order is processed. In a similar way a time interval for a production step stands for the real time interval where the production step is carried out. The time intervals for possible assignments of machines to production steps represent potential time intervals of production steps on resources.

- time intervals for orders:
  order_1, order_2, order_3
- time intervals for production steps:
  step_1.1, step_1.2, step_2.1, step_2.2, step_2.3, step_3.1, step_3.2
- time intervals for production steps on resources:
  step_1.1_a, step_1.1_b, step_1.2_b, step_2.1_a, step_2.1_b, step_2.2_b, step_2.3_b,
  step_2.3_c, step_3.1_c, step_3.2_c

Now we will specify, that every order includes its production steps by using the operator
includes:

⊂ (step_1.1, order_1), ⊂ (step_1.2, order_1)
⊂ (step_2.1, order_2), ⊂ (step_2.2, order_2), ⊂ (step_2.3, order_2)
⊂ (step_3.1, order_3), ⊂ (step_3.2, order_3)

Furthermore we will specify that intervals for productions with fixed machines are
equivalent to the intervals assigning the step to the only possible machine:

step_1.2 = step_1.2_a
step_2.2 = step_2.2_b
step_3.1 = step_3.1_c
step_3.2 = step_3.2_c

Production steps with alternative resources can be specified by the **or** operator:

OR(step_1.1, {step_1.1_a, step_1.1_b})

OR(step_2.1, {step_2.1_a, step_2.1_b})

OR(step_2.3, {step_2.3_b, step_2.3_c})

We have to specify that no production steps which are assigned to one resource may
run in parallel:

NOV(step_1.1_a, step_1.2_a, step_2.1_a)

NOV(step_1.1_b, step_2.1_b, step_2.2_b, step_2.3_b)

NOV(step_2.3_c, step_3.1_c, step_3.2_c)

Usually an order on a set of productions steps for one order is given. Here we may
consider the following order on production steps, which can be specified by the
operator **before**:

order 1:   *step_1.1 < step_1.2*
order 2:   *step_2.1 < step_2.3* and *step_2.2 < step_2.3*
order 3:   *step_3.1 < step_3.2*

Note, that step_2.2 and step_2.1 may run in parallel since no order on these steps has
been specified.

Up to now the due dates and the durations of production steps are not specified. This
information can be added as numerical constraints. We will specify the due dates of the
orders as soft constraints, because it is possible to specify due dates which cannot be
satisfied.

END(order_1) ≤ 7   (SOFT)

$END(order\_2) \le 11$ (SOFT)

$END(order\_3) \le 12$ (SOFT)

The duration of a production step cannot be specified for its time interval, because the execution duration of the step may depend on the resource. Therefore we will assign the durations to the intervals for the resource assignments. These durations have to be hard constraints:

$2 \le DURATION(step\_1.1\_a) \le 2$ (HARD)

$3 \le DURATION(step\_1.1\_b) \le 3$ (HARD)

$3 \le DURATION(step\_1.2\_a) \le 3$ (HARD)

$4 \le DURATION(step\_2.1\_a) \le 4$ (HARD)

$5 \le DURATION(step\_2.1\_b) \le 5$ (HARD)

$3 \le DURATION(step\_2.2\_b) \le 3$ (HARD)

$2 \le DURATION(step\_2.3\_b) \le 2$ (HARD)

$1 \le DURATION(step\_2.3\_c) \le 1$ (HARD)

$5 \le DURATION(step\_3.1\_c) \le 5$ (HARD)

$4 \le DURATION(step\_3.2\_c) \le 4$ (HARD)

A priority label is assigned to every interval which represents an order:

priority(order_1) = 1
priority(order_2) = 2
priority(order_3) = 3

These priorities specify, that the due date of order 3 is more important than the due date of order 2, and the due date of order 2 is more important than the due date of order 1.

Finally we have to choose a set of top intervals. For this example we will choose the intervals for the orders:

TOP : order_1, order_2, order_3

With this specification, the time intervals for the orders and the production steps have to be in the final plan. Also the intervals

step_1.2_a, step_2.2_b, step_3.1_c, step_3.2_c

have to be in the final plan, because they are equivalent to some production steps. From the following intervals, not all will occur in the final plan.

step_1.1_a, step_1.1_b, step_2.1_a, step_2.1_b, step_2.3_b, step_2.3_c

4-3. Generating and Optimizing Plans

After representing the plan with our language, a planning procedure has to be able to generate a correct plan from the representation. This task requires the following decisions:

- Choose an alternative for every operator **OR**.
- Choose a total order on all time intervals for a **NOV**–operator.
- Choose a start and finish time for every time interval.

The choices for the **OR** operator specify the resources and the choices for the **NOV** operator specify the order of the production steps on a resource. A choice for every **OR** and **NOV** operator specifies a partial order on all production steps and a duration for every step. From this partial order and the duration, one can directly derive the start and finish time for every step (see for example: [Falkenhausen 1968]). Therefore, it is not necessary for the planning procedure to assign start and finish times for the time intervals.

The decisions of the planning procedure can be represented by the language itself:

- If one chooses an alternative b_i for an **OR** relationship $or(a, \{ b_1, \ldots, b_n \})$, then the relationship $= (a, b_i)$ should be added.

- If one chooses a total order for a **NOV** relationship, then it can be represented by adding relationships with the operator $<$ for the intervals from the **NOV** relationship.

- Although it may not be necessary, one may represent decisions, which specify the start and finish times of time intervals, by numerical constraints.

In our example we may choose the resource a for the steps *step_1.1*, *step_2.1* and the resource c for the step *step_2.3*:

step_1.1 $=$ *step_1.1_a*

step_2.1 $=$ *step_2.1_a*

step_2.3 $=$ *step_2.3_c*

We also choose a total ordering for every **NOV** – operator:

step_2.1_a $<$ *step_1.1_a* $<$ *step_1.2_a*

step_3.1_c $<$ *step_3.2_c* $<$ *step_2.3_c*

From these decisision we can derive a production plan by assigning durations, start and finish times to every step. We represent these assignments by a net, where the nodes are the steps and the before operators are the edges. The duration of a step is given on the top and the start and finish time of a step are given on the bottom of its box:

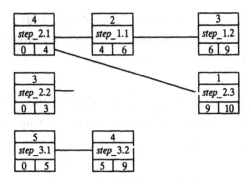

After assigning the durations, the start– and the finish times to every production step, the plan optimization procedure may start. This plan optimization will check all requirements which are not satisfied. In our case the latest finish time of 7 for order 1 has not been satisfied, because production step *step_1.2* of order 1 will be finished at 9. Here the plan optimization procedure should decrease the finish time of *step_1.2* without violating other latest finish time constraints.

In general a finish time of a production step may be decreased by decreasing its duration or by decreasing its start time. The only possible way for decreasing the duration of a step is to choose a faster resource. For decreasing the start time of the current step, one has to find a previous step for which the finish time is equal to the start time of the current step. In this case one has three different options:

- Decrease the finish time of a previous step .

- When the before operator between the current step and the previous step has been introduced by a planning procedure, then find a new ordering for the resource of the current step.

- When the before operator between the current step and the previous step has been introduced by a planning procedure, then find a new resource for the current or the previous step.

For our example the plan optimization procedure should try to reduce the finish time of interval *step_1.2*. Because the duration of this interval cannot be reduced (no other resource exists), one has to reduce the start time of this interval. For decreasing the start time of interval *step_1.2*, we have to consider a previous interval for which the finish time is equal to the start time of the current interval. In our case we get the interval *step_1.1*. Now the before operator between the interval *step_1.1* and *step_1.2* is not a planning decision, therefore we have to reduce the finish time of *step_1.1* for reducing the start time of *step_1.2*.

Again the duration of the considered interval *step_1.1* cannot be reduced because the chosen resource is already the fastest one (check **OR** operator and durations). Therefore one has to reduce the start time of this interval. The start time of this interval can be reduced by choosing a different resource for the previous interval *step_2.1*. Therefore one may remove the equivalent operator between the two intervals step_2.1 and step_2.1_a and add the following new relationship:

   step_2.1 = step_2.1_b

This new assignment requires that we specify an ordering for the NOV operator for resource *b*. For this resource one has to choose a total ordering for the intervals *step_2.1_b* and *step_2.2_b* as for example:

   step_2.2_b < step_2.1_b

From these modified decisions we can derive the following plan:

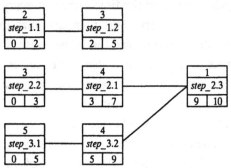

This plan satisfies all latest finish time requirements and therefore the plan optimization procedure may return it as the result.

In general the plan optimization procedure has to perform the following tasks:

- Find constraints which are not satisfied.
- Find decisions which should be altered for satisfying one constraint without violating others.
- Replace existing decisions by new decisions (delete and add **OR** and **before** operators).

Note:

- The plan can be modified locally by considering only some **NOV** and **OR** relationships! This is an essential feature for efficient plan optimization procedures.
- Sometimes a plan optimization procedure has to modify a big number of planning decisions for satisfying a requirement. The reason is, that a modification should not violate requirements, which were already satisfied.

5. Conclusion

We have introduced a language for representing planning problems, planning decisions and plans in one single formalism. This language supports the analysis and the modification of a plan, which are major tasks for a plan optimization procedure. Also the language allows to modify single decisions without modifying any other decisions. With this feature one can easily bound the search space of a plan optimization procedure, by restricting the number of decisions which are considered by the procedure.

Currently the language cannot represent resources with capacities. In future we will extend the language by replacing the **NOV** operator by a capacity operator. This capacity operator requires new language constructs for representing planning decisions. With these constructs one has to be able to specify an ordering of production steps on a resource, where some of the step may run in parallel.

References

[Allen 1983] James F. Allen:
Maintaining Knowledge About Temporal Intervals
Communications of the ACM **26** 11, November 1983, pp. 832 – 843

[DLR 1989]
D–PAF: German Processing and Archiving Facility
Deutsche Forschungsanstalt für Luft- und Raumfahrt, Oberpfaffenhofen 1989

[Dornier 1990]
TINA: Time Line Assistant, User Manual
Dornier, Friederichshafen 1990

[Falkenhausen 1968] Falkenhausen, Hasso v.:
Prinzipien und Rechenverfahren der Netzplantechnik
Kiel 1968

[Fox, Sadeh, Baykan 1989] Mark S. Fox, Norman Sadeh, Can Baykan:
Constrained Heuristic Search
Proceedings of the International Joint Conference on Artificial Intelligence, Detroit, August 1989

[Fox 1990]: Mark S. Fox:
Constraint Guided Scheduling: A Short History of Research at CMU
to appear in: Computers and History

[Göbel, Rodosek 1990]: Göbel R., Rodosek R.:
A Language for Representing Planning Problems – Language Description
DLR Internal Paper, Oberpfaffenhofen 1990

[Kanal, Kumar 1988]: Kanal L., Kumar V.:
Search in Artificial Intelligence
Springer Verlag, New York 1988

[KEE 1990]:
KEE Scheduler Booster Module: Reference and User Manual
IntelliCorp Inc., Mountain View 1990

[Kellner 1990]: Kellner A.:
MARS: A Generic Mission Planning Tool
Proceedings of the First International Symposium on Ground Data Systems for Spacecraft Control, Darmstadt 1990

Towards a Theory of Simultaneous Actions

Gerd Große
FG Intellektik
TH Darmstadt
Alexanderstr. 10
6100 Darmstadt
Germany

Richard Waldinger*
Artificial Intelligence Center
SRI International
333 Ravenswood Ave.
Menlo Park, Ca 94025
U.S.A.

Abstract

We will lay down a model of concurrency for planning problems. The model will be expressive enough for representing real simultaneity of primitive actions without getting too complicated for the plan synthesis process. The model will be described in detail and its use in respect to the synthesis of terminating plans is demonstrated in an example.

Key words and phrases. Plan synthesis, concurrency, theorem proving, situational logic.

1 Introduction

There are two main streams in representing concurrency. The first one is the *interleaving model*, in which parallelism is not considered primitive but reducible to nondeterminism. The parallel execution of programs generates nondeterministically the same computation as some linear interleaving of the atomic actions of the programs. Hoare's CSP or Milner's CCS are well-known examples of this kind of model [H 78], [Mi 80]. A CSP-like model in connection with some kind of temporal logic was successfully used for the synthesis of concurrent programs [CE 81], [MWo 84].

The second model results by considering parallelism as primitive and the use of some partial order. This relation expresses whether a certain action necessarily precedes another one. Examples of the second model are Petri-nets or Pratt's Pomsets [R 85], [Pr 86]. The reasoning process, on the other hand, seems to be very difficult.

However, a large class of possible world behaviors, e.g., the ones which need explicit simultaneous actions, cannot be represented within either of the two models. For instance, suppose a large table with a glass of water on it is to be lifted. Because of the size of the table, this task requires two (or more) actors for lifting. In order to keep the water in the glass, all actors have to lift at exactly the same time; otherwise the glass would fall. This example requires a theory of simultaneous actions.

In the interleaving model explicit simultaneity is excluded, because all actions happen in a linear ordering. We do not want to express that the two lifting tasks can happen in either order, but that they happen at exactly the same time. The use of a partial ordering does not represent simultaneity either. Here it is only possible to express that none of the two actions has to precede the other one. This, however, is certainly not the same as simultaneity.

---

*This research is supported in part by the National Science Foundation under Grant CCR-8904809.

Pednault's technique for describing multiagent domains does not solve the problem either [Ped 86]. He constructed at first a sequential plan and searched afterwards for sequences of actions which can be executed in parallel. A sequence of two actions may be parallelized if the result of executing both one at a time is independent on the execution ordering. This representation, however, is not sufficient for our purposes since we are interested in additional effects caused by the simultaneous execution of actions. Moreover Pednault's condition for the introduction of simultaneity is insufficient. It may happen that actions cannot be executed simultaneously even though their sequential execution is possible in either order and yields the same result.

A theory rich enough for representing simultaneity is Allen's interval logic [A 84]. In this approach all possible relations of two actions can be described in terms of the time interval in which they happen. However, as shown by Pelavin, the reasoning process within this theory seems to be quite cumbersome [Pel 88].

Georgeff has recognized this dilemma and proposed a model that allows simultaneous actions and seems to be adequate for reasoning [G 87a], [G 87b]. In the present paper, we want to propose a similar model, which has much better computational features for the synthesis of plans. Moreover we connected the model with an existing program and plan synthesizer, i.e., the one from Manna and Waldinger [MW 80], [MW 87]. The yielded plans which contain simultaneous actions have obviously two advantages: Firstly, these plans can be shorter than plans in which actions happen sequentially, because some of these may now be executed in parallel. And secondly, many problems, e.g., the example with the glass on the table, are not solvable without explicit simultaneity as provided in our approach.

The content of the paper is as follows. In Chapter 2, the model will be explained in detail. Afterwards, in Chapter 3, we introduce an example world in which simultaneous actions are possible. The world will consist of a small keyboard where the pressing and releasing of arbitrary keys can be executed in parallel. All necessary axioms are also given. In Chapter 4, the use of the model in respect to the synthesis of a terminating plan is illustrated. The planning problem is taken from the keyboard example. The last chapter contains the conclusion.

2 A Model of Simultaneous Actions

We want to represent an arbitrary world by states which change after the occurrence of actions. An action always results in a state with different properties. The states and actions will be described by first-order predicate logic formulas.

Each action will be described by one action axiom. It is of the form of an implication, i.e., a precondition implies a conclusion. In order to apply the action, the precondition of the action axiom has to be true at the current state. After the execution the conclusion will be true in the successive state.

The general form of an axiom describing the action a is

$$(\forall s)(\forall \bar{x}) \left(\begin{array}{c} p(\bar{x}, s) \wedge possible(\{a(\bar{x})\}) \\ \rightarrow \\ \exists s'(c(\bar{x}, s')) \end{array} \right).$$

In this formula $\bar{x}$ denotes the objects to which the action a is applied. Precondition and conclusion are named p and c, respectively. The *possible*-predicate ensures that the action can actually be applied upon the given objects. This will be discussed in more detail later on. The state s' will later be referred to as $s; a(\bar{x})$. The operator ; composes a state and an action and yields the state after the execution of the action. This is explained precisely by Manna and Waldinger [MW 87].

In order to allow simultaneity, we introduce a concurrency operator, denoted by $\|$. Furthermore, we let the set of actions form a commutative semi group under the concurrency operator. It means, that the concurrent execution of two actions yields a new (composed) action which is of the same general form. Furthermore the set of actions obeys the laws of associativity and commutativity under the concurrency operator.

The composition of two actions has, firstly, to contain both p-preconditions and, secondly, it has to be ensured that their parallel composition is possible at all. The conclusion is then the conjunction of the single c-conclusions. It is important that the conclusion of the primitive action axioms consists only of predicates which are always true after the execution of the action. It means the conclusion is true independent on possible other actions that occur simultaneously. All other effects which also occur after the execution of several actions in parallel are represented by effect axioms. These will be explained later on.

Intuitively, we have two actions which can both be applied at the current state. For both separately, we know that the execution will result in a state. Since the parallel composition is allowed by the *possible*-predicate, we can say that there also exists a state in which the composed action will result. In this state both c-predicates are true. Thus the composition of two action axioms yields (after appropriate renaming) the following axiom:

$$(\forall s)(\forall \bar{x}_1)(\forall \bar{x}_2) \left(\begin{array}{c} p_1(\bar{x}_1, s) \wedge p_2(\bar{x}_2, s) \wedge \\ possible(\{a_1(\bar{x}_1)\} \uplus \{a_2(\bar{x}_2)\}) \\ \rightarrow \\ \exists s' \left((c_1(\bar{x}_1, s') \wedge c_2(\bar{x}_2, s')) \right) \end{array} \right)$$

where $\uplus$ is the multiset union of actions. The state variable s' denotes the state yielded after the application of $a_1(\bar{x}) \| a_2(\bar{x})$ to the state s. This formula again has to be considered as a new action of the form:

$$(\forall s)(\forall \bar{x}) \left(\begin{array}{c} p(\bar{x}, s) \wedge possible(\{a(\bar{x})\}) \\ \rightarrow \\ \exists s' \, c(\bar{x}, s') \end{array} \right)$$

where

$$\bar{x} = \bar{x}_1 \cup \bar{x}_2$$

$$p(\bar{x}, s) = p_1(\bar{x}_1, s) \wedge p_2(\bar{x}_2, s)$$

$$c(\bar{x}, s') = c_1(\bar{x}_1, s') \wedge c_2(\bar{x}_2, s')$$

$$\{a(\bar{x})\} = \{a_1(\bar{x}_1)\} \uplus \{a_2(\bar{x}_2)\}$$

It is straightforward to show that the actions build a commutative semi group under the concurrency operator: The actions are closed under composition as shown above. The laws for associativity and commutativity are also valid, because the $\uplus$ and $\wedge$ operators are known to be associative and commutative.

The difference of this method compared with Georgeff's approach is that the parallel execution of actions is a state function. The former state will result in exactly one new state. This we achieve by composing all actions which happen at a given state to one action. Applying this composed action to the state yields the new state.

Georgeff, on the other hand, has used state relations for describing actions. It means that a given state will change to one out of a set of possible new states by the specific action. Which state the resulting new state is depends on what other actions may happen in parallel. The consequence is that he does not need additional effect axioms. The use of his approach is not more expressive than the one proposed here. In addition to that the plan synthesis process in his description will be more complicated. By composing several actions to one we reduce the set of possible next states also to one. This step simplifies the following reasoning process so far that we can use a modified version of Manna and Waldinger's *deductive tableau* method for synthesizing sequential plans.

2.1 The Effect Axioms

Unfortunately, the composition of actions is not sufficient for predicting all effects caused by several simultaneously occurring actions. The predicate in the conclusion of an axiom expresses only what is necessarily true in the state after the execution of the action. However, there are effects which are not explicitly connected to an action. It means that an arbitrary effect occurs sometimes but not always when an action was executed before. The effects are caused by certain other predicates which may also be true. For instance, if one actor lifts a table at one side, a glass standing on the table would fall. On the other hand, if another actor lifted the table at the opposite side with the same speed and to the same height at the same moment the glass would not move. Such situations will be represented by additional effect axioms. These distinguish then whether only one or both sides of the table are lifted and give the correct behavior for the glass on the table. The general form of an effect axiom is as follows:

$$(\forall s)(\forall \bar{x}) \left(\begin{array}{c} p(\bar{x}, s) \\ \rightarrow \\ c(\bar{x}, s) \end{array} \right)$$

The meaning is that the c-predicate is true in state s if the p-condition is true at s. Note that the effects occur at the same state.

2.2 The Possibility of an Action

There is furthermore a need for a predicate that states what actions can be simultaneously executed on what objects. For instance, a robot cannot walk forward and backward at the same time, even though both actions are separately possible. Also there might be tasks which cannot be carried out by only one action, for example, the lifting of a heavy block, which can only be done by two or more weak actors. And finally we want to illustrate why Pednault's approach is insufficient. Suppose two agents have to carry two boxes, a and b, from one room to the next. Unfortunately, the connecting door is too small for letting both agents through at the same time. Then sequentially the task of bringing firstly box a and then b is possible and will have the same result as bringing firstly b and then a. However, the simultaneous execution is not possible and should therefore be prevented in a suitable way.

For all these conflict situations the user has to give suitable axioms, which prevent impossible action compositions. The predicate regarding that is dependent upon the actions and their objects. It does not depend on the current state, because this information should be formulated within the p-precondition instead. Thus, our system provides the following predicate:

$$possible(\{action\ multiset\})$$

The action multiset contains a precise set of actions that can be carried out simultaneously. It means that no action can be added or omitted; either could make the predicate false. The use of a multiset is to handle cases where two or more identical actions are needed to perform a task, e.g., the lifting of a heavy object.

It might be possible to simplify the above predicate but in the last consequence the user has to give the necessary information anyway. Every current reasoning system is overchallenged otherwise.

3 An Example

We want to illustrate the theory with a small example: A keyboard consisting of two characters, a and b, and one *shift*-key. Simultaneity arises here when typing a capital character, e.g., A, on our monitor. This may be done by pressing the keys for *shift* and a at exactly the same time. It is in our intention to keep the example as simple as possible. Therefore we do not give a complete set of axioms, but only the ones which are necessary. Moreover the described keyboard behaves a little bit unusual compared with common ones. This is caused by the attempt to keep the axioms simple. Since the solutions for the conflict problem of simultaneous actions and the frame problem are not in the scope of the paper, we keep these parts also very short. The model can easily be extended to a larger number of keys.

For the object descriptions we will introduce two sets of keys, the set C, which consists of the characters a and b, and the set K, which consists of C and the *shift* -key. The following list will be used as axioms in our system:

$$\forall x \, (x = x) \tag{1}$$

$$\forall x \, (x \in C \equiv (x = a \lor x = b)) \tag{2}$$

$$\forall x \, (x = b \rightarrow x \neq a) \tag{3}$$

$$\forall x \, (x \in K \equiv (x = shift \lor x \in C)) \tag{4}$$

For describing the states two predicates will be used: The first one is $pressed(x, s)$ which expresses whether or not a key x is pressed in a state s. The second one is $printed(x, s)$ which means that the character x appears on the screen at state s. All further predicate symbols have their common meaning. In addition to that we will use the function $capital(x)$, which yields capital-x.

We shall permit two actions: That are pressing and releasing a key in a state s, denoted $s; press(x)$ and $s; release(x)$, respectively. By skolemizing the action axiom we introduce a new function $g(s, \bar{x})$. This function g will be denoted $s; a(\bar{x})$, where a is the action described by the axiom. Hence we introduce the following axioms:

$$(\forall s)(\forall x) \left(\begin{array}{c} x \in K \land \neg pressed(x, s) \land possible(\{press(x)\}) \\ \rightarrow \\ pressed(x, s; press(x)) \end{array} \right) \tag{5}$$

$$(\forall s)(\forall x) \left(\begin{array}{c} x \in K \land pressed(x, s) \land possible(\{release(x)\}) \\ \rightarrow \\ \neg pressed(x, s; release(x)) \end{array} \right)$$

The *press*-action is executable if the object is an element of the set of keys, the object was not pressed in the current state and the action is applicable to the object. As the resulting direct effect, the object x is pressed in the state following the execution of the action at state s. The *release*-action has to be interpreted similarly.

As mentioned above, we are interested in executing two *press*-actions simultaneously. Hence, we could allow that two *press*-actions are always allowed to execute simultaneously as long as the keys are different. In our synthesis in the next chapter, however, it is only required that the pressing of the *a*-key and the *shift*-key can be done at the same time. Hence, it is sufficient to use the following predicate as an axiom:

$$possible(\{press(a), press(shift)\}) \tag{6}$$

The effect that a pressed character appears on the screen should not be written as an action axiom. It is more elegant to formulate it as an effect, that occurs if certain predicates are true. For instance, if only the key a is pressed in state s, then an a will appear on the screen at the same moment.

Later on, we will need an axiom for the appearance of a capital letter on the screen. It will be of the form:

$$(\forall s)(\forall x)(\forall y) \left(\begin{array}{c} x \in C \wedge \\ pressed(x, s) \wedge pressed(shift, s) \wedge \\ ((y \in C \wedge y \neq x) \rightarrow \neg pressed(y, s)) \\ \rightarrow \\ printed(capital(x), s) \end{array} \right) \tag{7}$$

where the predicate $printed(capital(x), s)$ denotes the appearance of the capital of x on the screen in state s. The implication takes care that no other keys are pressed at the same time. If we used a more complex description here, our keyboard would be more similar to the common ones.

The analogous action for pressing an arbitrary character is:

$$(\forall s)(\forall x)(\forall y) \left(\begin{array}{c} x \in C \wedge pressed(x, s) \wedge \\ ((y \in K \wedge y \neq x) \rightarrow \neg pressed(y, s)) \\ \rightarrow \\ printed(x, s) \end{array} \right)$$

A well-known difficulty when reasoning with simultaneous actions is the frame or persistence problem. It is the question what remains true after the occurrence of an action. The solution of this problem, however, is not in the scope of this paper. Therefore we just add an appropriate axiom that satisfies our upcoming requirements. In particular, it has to be proven that if the *b*-key is not pressed before the simultaneous action of pressing the *a*-key and the *shift*-key, then it remains unpressed after the occurred action. This will be expressed by the following axiom:

$$(\forall s) \left(\begin{array}{c} \neg pressed(b, s) \\ \rightarrow \\ \neg pressed(b, s; press(a) \parallel press(shift)) \end{array} \right) \tag{8}$$

4 Plan Synthesis

In the present paper, we restrict ourselves to terminating planning problems. Then the plan construction can be seen as the decomposition of a specification to a plan consisting of (simultaneous) actions leading from the initial state s_0 to some final state. This will be done by formulating the specification as a theorem and proving the theorem to be valid. The theorem is valid if and only if a plan exists. As a by-product of the proof the successful plan will be developed by the substitutions used in the proof. An appropriate interactive theorem prover is the one developed by Manna and Waldinger which is used for the derivation of sequential programs and plans [MW 80], [MW 87]. We will focus only on the introduction of a simultaneous action in the synthesis process. All other complex proof steps, e.g., the introduction of conditional clauses or recursive loops, can be used as described in the references.

The reasoning process for the keyboard example would be as follows. In order to get a capital letter, e.g., A, on the screen we have to prove the following specification or goal:

$$f(a) \Leftarrow \text{find a plan } z \text{ such that } printed(capital(a), s_0; z)$$

We will start with the following row:

Assertion	Goal	Plan
	$printed(capital(a), s_0; z)$	$s_0; z$

Now, effect axiom 7 can be used to establish the predicate in the goal column.

Assertion	Goal	Plan
$x \in C \wedge$ $pressed(x, s) \wedge pressed(shift, s) \wedge$ $[y \in C \wedge y \neq x \rightarrow \neg pressed(y, s)]$ $\rightarrow$ $printed(capital(x), s)$		

In order to unify both *printed*-predicates, we have to carry out two substitutions before:

$$\{x \leftarrow a, s \leftarrow s_0; z\}$$

By resolving the *printed*-predicates we will get the following new row:

Assertion	Goal	Plan
	$a \in C \wedge$ $pressed(a, s_0; z) \wedge pressed(shift, s_0; z) \wedge$ $[y \in C \wedge y \neq a \rightarrow \neg pressed(y, s_0; z)]$	$s_0; z$

In the next step we will compose a *press(a)*-action axiom with a *press(shift)*-action axiom via the described method to a new action axiom. The composition task can be seen as a meta-theoretical step. This step is the only modification of the *deductive tableau* method. Therefore all properties of this synthesizer remain to be the same. By introducing this composed action, we will derive a shorter plan for solving our problem. The primitive action (row 1) will be used twice to compose the new action (row 2):

Assertion	Goal	Plan
$x \in K \wedge \neg pressed(x,s) \wedge$ $possible(\{press(x)\})$ $\rightarrow$ $pressed(x, s; press(x))$		
$x_1 \in K \wedge \neg pressed(x_1, s) \wedge$ $x_2 \in K \wedge \neg pressed(x_2, s) \wedge$ $possible(\{press(x_1)\} \uplus \{press(x_2)\})$ $\rightarrow$ $pressed(x_1, s; press(x_1) \parallel press(x_2)) \wedge$ $pressed(x_2, s; press(x_1) \parallel press(x_2))$		

Note that we had to rename the variables in an appropriate manner.

The application of this axiom on the last goal clause introduces the first plan step. The unification will be carried out with the following substitutions:

$$\{x_1 \leftarrow a, x_2 \leftarrow shift, s \leftarrow s_0, z \leftarrow press(a) \parallel press(shift)\} \ .$$

This step unifies the two *pressed*-predicates at once and leads to:

Assertion	Goal	Plan
	$a \in C \wedge a \in K \wedge shift \in K \wedge$ $[y \in C \wedge y \neq a \rightarrow$ $\neg pressed(y, s_0; press(a) \parallel press(shift))] \wedge$ $\neg pressed(a, s_0) \wedge \neg pressed(shift, s_0) \wedge$ $possible(\{press(a)\} \uplus \{press(shift)\})$	$s_0;$ $press(a) \parallel$ $press(shift)$

All the substitutions were also applied to the associated plan clause.

After the application of the model description axioms (1, 2 and 4) and the possible axiom (6), the reasoning process yields the following row:

Assertion	Goal	Plan
	$[y \in C \wedge y \neq a \rightarrow$ $\neg pressed(y, s_0; press(a) \parallel press(shift))] \wedge$ $\neg pressed(a, s_0) \wedge \neg pressed(shift, s_0)$	$s_0;$ $press(a) \parallel$ $press(shift)$

The next step is the proof of persistence that all untouched keys remain in the same position. First we transform the goal clause by using the model description axioms (2 and 3) and some techniques belonging to the deductive tableau method to:

Assertion	Goal	Plan
	$[y \neq b \vee$ $\neg pressed(b, s_0; press(a) \parallel press(shift))] \wedge$ $\neg pressed(a, s_0) \wedge \neg pressed(shift, s_0)$	$s_0;$ $press(a) \parallel$ $press(shift)$

Then we apply the persistence axiom (8) to get:

Assertion	Goal	Plan
	$\neg pressed(b, s_0) \wedge$ $\neg pressed(a, s_0) \wedge$ $\neg pressed(shift, s_0)$	$s_0;$ $press(a) \parallel$ $press(shift)$

Dependent on what is known about the initial state, the process continues or as here will be shortened by the introduction of the following axiom expressing that no key is pressed in the initial state s_0:

Assertion	Goal	Plan
$x \in K \rightarrow \neg pressed(x, s_0)$		

Using this information we can conclude the following final row:

Assertion	Goal	Plan
	$true$	s_0; $press(a) \parallel$ $press(shift)$

The resulting plan leading from the initial state s_0 to the final state in which an A is printed on the screen is:

$$f(a) = press(a) \parallel press(shift)$$

This is obviously a correct result, but not the only one. It is also possible to meet the specification by pressing the two keys, a and $shift$, after each other. All alternative plans, however, have one thing in common: the sequence of actions is longer than the one we developed.

By modifying our example world slightly, we can easily build specifications, where simultaneous actions are necessary for every correct plan. For instance, we may define that printing an A on the screen can only be done when no key is pressed and the next action applied is the simultaneous pressing of a and $shift$.

5   Conclusion

We built a theory in which we are able to represent simultaneous actions. The advantage of this new model is that the plan synthesis process is not more complicated as in models without simultaneous actions. This was achieved by the development of a theory for composing actions. The use of this approach was illustrated in a small example. In the next future the extension to non-terminating reactive systems is planned.

References

[A 84]   J.F. Allen. *Towards a General Theory of Action and Time*, AI Journal 23, 1984

[CE 81]   E.M. Clarke, E.A. Emerson. *Design and Synthesis of Synchronization Skeletons from Branching-Time Temporal Logic*, Logics of Programs, Springer LNCS 131, 1981

[G 87a]   M.P. Georgeff. *Actions, Processes, and Causality*, Tech. Note 404, SRI International, 1987

[G 87b]   M.P. Georgeff. *Many Agents are better than one*, Tech. Note 417, SRI International, 1987

[H 78]   C.A.R. Hoare. *Communicating Sequential Processes*, CACM, 1978

[Mi 80]   R. Milner. *A Calculus of Communicating Systems*, Springer LNCS 92, 1980

[MW 80]   Z. Manna, R. Waldinger. *A Deductive Approach to Program Synthesis*, ACM Transactions on Programming Languages and Systems, 1980

[MW 87]   Z. Manna, R. Waldinger. *How to Clear a Block*, J. o. Automated Reasoning, 1987

[MWo 84] Z. Manna, P. Wolper. *Synthesis of Communicating Processes from Temporal-Logic Specifications*, ACM Transactions on Programming Languages and Systems, 1984

[Pel 88] R.N. Pelavin. *A Formal Approach to Planning with Concurrent Actions and External Events*, Ph.D. thesis, University of Rochester, New York, 1988

[Ped 86] E. Pednault. *Formulating Multiagent, Dynamic-World Problems in the Classical Planning Framework*, Proceedings of the Workshop 'Reasoning about Actions and Plans', Georgeff and Lansky (eds.), 1986

[Pr 86] V.R. Pratt. *Modeling Concurrency with Partial Orders*, Int. J. Parallel Programming, 1986

[R 85] W. Reisig. *Petri Nets: An Introduction*, Springer, 1985

MTMM — Correcting and Extending Time Map Management[*]

Stefan Materne, Joachim Hertzberg

German National Research Center for Computer Science (GMD)
Schloß Birlinghoven
5205 Sankt Augustin 1, F.R.G.
email: hertz@gmdzi.gmd.de

Abstract

We present the concept of the deductive temporal data base MTMM, that corrects and extends Dean's [85] TMM in a number of aspects, allowing complete and consistent temporal inferences from a temporal model that may be given in a quantitative or qualitative way. The user is allowed to incorporate a certain form of inconsistency in the time map; we will demonstrate that this is a useful feature. Moreover, the user may withdraw any information at any time. The expressiveness of the temporal logic of the MTMM is equivalent to convex subsets of Allen's relations.

We present the basics of the MTMM, going into the concepts of persistence, persistence clipping, and validity in a bit more detail.

1   Background

In everyday life, few facts are timelessly true. This is, however, not mirrored in straight-forward—or somewhat naive—representations of real world scenarios like predicate calculus or PROLOG, which, first of all, treat everything as eternal verities. Dealing with change over time lies at the heart of some classes of AI applications like planning or reasoning about processes. Consequently, there are approaches to capturing change in different frameworks:

- logical frameworks, e.g., situation calculus [McCarthy/Hayes 69] and possible models [Hanks/McDermott 85], [Ginsberg/Smith 88],
- planning, e.g., adding and deleting facts in STRIPS [Fikes/Nilsson 71], or
- qualitative reasoning with process oriented [Forbus 84], state oriented [deKleer/ Brown 84], and interval based [Voß/Linster 89] approaches.

In our work, we deal with Dean's [Dean 85, Dean/McDermott 87] *time map management system* (TMM), where a *time map* is a data base containing facts and temporal information about these facts. Dean has done pioneering work in that area; as far as can be judged from his publications, however, he seems to have come to a number of pragmatic decisions concerning

---

[*] Work partly done in the joint project TASSO, supported by Fed. Min. for Research and Technology, grant no. ITW 8900 A7. TASSO is also part of the GMD "Leitvorhaben" Assisting Computer (AC)

Hans Voß co-authored a companion paper [Materne/Hertzberg/Voß 90] that shares some amount of work with this one. Thanks to Tom Gordon and Hans Werner Güsgen for reading earlier versions of this paper.

both his concept of time map management and its implementation in the TMM that make it not obvious how to generalize his ideas.

In [Materne 90], it is attempted to correct and to generalize some of Dean's ideas found wanting—or, at least, to make some hidden assumptions explicit—, resulting in another system for time map management: the MTMM. In this paper, we summarize its key issues, thereby presenting a constructive critique of TMM's reasoning. (In the following, we presume familiarity with Dean's work.)

We do *not* discuss here the question of how to integrate the MTMM into application systems, in particular into a planning system. Considering planning, there are two problems within a planner that can be solved by the MTMM:

- planning with time: a self-contained system for planning without quantitative time is extended by the MTMM for handling time; this results in a DEVISER-like [Vere 83] functionality with an EXCALIBUR-like [Drabble 88] architecture.
- managing goal achievement and conflict: the planner is based on the MTMM that has to take care of the (partial) task order in the plan.

These questions are discussed at length in [Materne 90].

The paper is organized as follows. In the next section, we will present the basic example problem used throughout the paper. Then, we will define the basic notions of time map management in a (moderately) formal style. After that, we go into the concepts of persistence clipping, persistence, and validity in a bit more detail. Finally, we summarize some MTMM features, resulting in a brief characterization of its expressiveness as compared to Allen's [83] temporal logics.

2 The example problem

Vacationer Timm, lying on the beach, is considering his program for tomorrow: he wants to water ski for 1 to 1.5 hours, depending on his physical condition then; he thinks he will arrive at the beach at 10:30; he has to be back at the hotel by 1:00 in order not to miss the lunch. There are two boatmen in question for hauling him:

- Miguel arrives every day between 11:00 and 11:30 at the beach and will stay between 3 and 6 hours, i.e., he is available until 2:00, at least. He has to leave by 5:30 as he has to cook in the local *bodega*.
- Pedro is available from 8:30; he is guaranteed to stay for 2 hours, at least. However, his mother-in-law Carmen may arrive wishing Pedro to drive her into town immediately, seizing him for at least 1 hour. All that is known about her arrival is that she likes to sleep long, and Pedro has asked his wife to keep her at home until 10:30. On the other hand, Carmen is not sure to arrive at any specific time; maybe she won't come at all, and Pedro may be on the beach until dusk. In addition to the Carmen problem, Pedro may decide by himself to go home at some time later than 10:30 for the rest of the day, independent of the possibility that Carmen might arrive later.

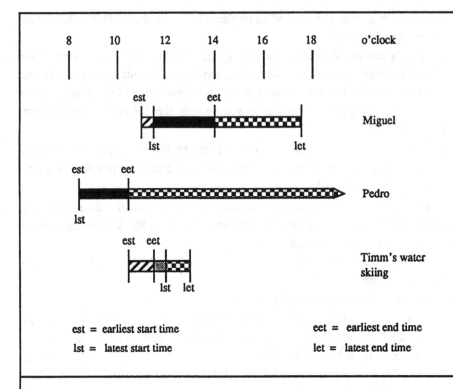

Figure 1 The availabilities of the boatmen and
Timm's water skiing plans

Timm has to decide today which boatman to hire for tomorrow. Timm is guaranteed to water ski with Miguel as long as he likes, which is not so sure with Pedro; on the other hand, he cannot start water skiing before 11:00 with Miguel, which could be possible with Pedro. Consider further that Pedro may be a lot cheaper, and you see there is a problem to solve. (We will refer to all this as the *basic example* later.)

In Figure 1, we show the respective availabilities of Miguel and Pedro[1]: The boatmen become available between the earliest and the latest start times indicated by their respective bars (hatched areas); they are sure to be available between the latest start and the earliest end times (black areas); their availability ends between their earliest and latest end times (checkered areas). Timm's water skiing plans are represented, too. The earliest end time is earlier than the latest start time (dotted area). In this time interval, e.g., at 11:45, he is possibly already water skiing, he possibly has finished already, or none of both.

---

[1]It is difficult to present *all* sorts of temporal information in *one* graphic. Our form of presentation shows most relevant information except, e.g., for the maximal duration of facts like Timm's desire to water ski for at most 1.5 hours and minimal durations like Miguel's availability for 3 hours at least.

Let us now develop the equipment to describe and solve this problem by introducing a few definitions and "language macros".

3 Basic definitions

Our concept of time map management is founded on the idea of point-based, continuous time, i.e., the primitive unit is a *point of time* or *point*, for short. An essential feature in time maps are relations between points. With $\mathfrak{R}^\infty:=\mathfrak{R}\cup\{+\infty,-\infty\}$ and obvious rules for extending arithmetics of $\mathfrak{R}$ on $\pm\infty$ we define

Definition 1 (Temporal relation): A temporal relation between two points p and q is a pair $[x,y]$, $x\leq y$, of numbers in $\mathfrak{R}^\infty$; x (y, resp.) is to be interpreted as a lower (upper) bound of the temporal distance between p and q. p (q, resp.) is called start (end) point of the temporal relation. The temporal relation $[x,y]$ is called exaxt if $x=y$; otherwise it is called vague.

We will sloppily speak of *relation* instead of temporal relation, whenever this causes no confusion. A temporal relation is a convex subset of $\mathfrak{R}^\infty$, containing the effective temporal distance between the two points in question. For example, the relation between the two points "start" and "end of Miguel's availability" is [3,6], interpreting numbers as hours; this relation is obviously vague. We express absolute time information by a temporal relation to a reference point. E.g., the relation between the reference point 0:00 and the start of Pedro's availability at 8:30 is [8.5,8.5], which is an exact relation.

Note that a relation is directed from its start to its end point. For every relation, there is a unique, equivalent relation for the reverse direction, which is obtained by applying the *reversity rule*, where $-[x,y]$ is a shorthand for reversing the relation $[x,y]$:

$$-[x,y] = [-y,-x].$$

In an *exact* relation, the lower bound equals the upper bound. Otherwise, the relation is *vague*, like the relation concerning the duration of Miguel's availability.

Some relations are explicitly given as parts of the domain description by the user; these are called *constraints*. The temporal information about the duration of Miguel's availability, e.g., is a constraint. Some relations are *derived* from other relations, like the relation [2.5,3] for the points "Start of Pedro's availability" and "Start of Miguel's availability".

By connecting points, the constraints constitute a *constraint network* which spans the whole set of relations. Based on this network, the relation between two points not directly connected by constraints can be calculated. This is done using the obvious rules for adding the upper and lower bounds, respectively, of chains of constraints, regarding their orientation. There may be more than one relation between two points. The relation between the start of Pedro's availability and the start of Carmen's seizing Pedro (her arrival, for short), e.g., may be defined by the two relations $[0,\infty]$ (Carmen may arrive at any time after Pedro's arrival) and $[2,\infty]$ (Pedro has taken care that she won't arrive before 10:30). Hence, single relations don't unambiguously define the temporal distance between two points, and we need:

Definition 2 (Minimized temporal relation): The *minimized temporal relation* between two points is a pair $<x,y>$ of numbers in $\Re^\infty$; x (y, resp.) is the lower (upper) bound of the temporal distance between the two points. The lower (upper) bound of the minimized temporal relation is the maximum (minimum) of the lower (upper) bounds of all temporal relations between the two points.

We will speak of *minimized relation* instead of minimized temporal relation, for short. Minimized relations may be exact or vague, analogously to relations. The minimized relation between the start of Pedro's availability and Carmen's arrival, e.g., is the vague pair $<2,\infty>$. Note that the minimized relation between any two points is unique because it can be interpreted as finding a locally consistent solution in a constraint network using filtering, which is known to yield unique results under certain restrictions [Güsgen/Hertzberg 88]; this is explained in more detail in [Materne 90].

Now, we can define a recurring phenomenon in time maps, namely, inconsistency. Note, however, that there will be another type of inconsistency (token inconsistency) below.

Definition 3 (Constraint inconsistency) A set of constraints is called *inconsistent* iff for at least one pair of points involved with the minimized relation $<x,y>$ holds $x>y$.

Assume, e.g., there is another constraint stating that Miguel is available for 1 hour, at least, and 2 hours, at most. Together with the old constraint [3,6] we get $<3,2>$ for the minimized relation between the start and the end of Miguel's availability, which we would have to interpret as: he is at least available for 3 hours, and at most for 2 hours. (MTMM handles this type of inconsistency by forbidding to introduce a constraint that would result in a constraint inconsistency.)

Now we can define time maps. Note, however, that this definition is slightly different from Dean's; his time maps correspond more closely to our constraint networks.

Definition 4 (Time map) Let Π be a set of points, Δ be the set of minimized relations between points in Π. A *time map* is the directed graph consisting of the nodes Π and the edges Δ.

A time map is called *vague*, if it contains at least one vague minimized relation.

Different to Dean's concept, we do *not* differentiate between facts and events. Let aside ontological intricacies, this difference has proven unnecessary for the MTMM; this is discussed in more detail in [Materne 90]. By the way, from the examples reported in the literature, we could not see that such a difference is mirrored in the TMM implementation.

To represent facts and events we use *token types* and *tokens* in the usual, i.e., Dean-style way. For example, the very fact that *Miguel is available* is a token type; the fact instance that *Miguel is available tomorrow from between 11:00 and 11:30 until between 2:00 and 5:30* is represented as a token. A token has a start and an end point, where the former must not be later than the latter, in absolute time. The minimized relation corresponding to the pair of points *Start* and *End of token T* will be called *token interval* of T, for short.

We, then, come to a tiny yet important detail: Is the fact represented by a token valid at the points corresponding to the token boundaries? The answer is, of course: it depends! There are the usual distinctions between open and closed intervals, and we have

Definition 5 (Boundary type): The *boundary type* of a token is one of CC, CO, OC, OO, to be interpreted as closed/closed (both start and end point are parts of the token), closed/open (the start point, but not the end point, is part of the token), and so on.

Note that Dean does *not* introduce boundary types; he introduces the values *pos-tiny* and *neg-tiny* instead, and we assume that these values could somehow be used for modeling different boundary types. However, we don't use them as we don't see a neat way to extend real arithmetic accordingly.

A key problem in time map management are overlapping contradictory tokens. We will say that two token types are *contradictory* if they are asserted to be so. Two tokens are called contradictory if their respective types are contradictory. As to overlapping of tokens, consider the following definition:

Definition 6 (definite/non-definite overlap) Two tokens are said to *definitely overlap* iff there is at least one point in time (even if regarding vagueness) at which both tokens are certainly valid. If there is no such point enforcing overlap, but if the existence of a common point cannot be excluded, then the two tokens are said to *non-definitely overlap*. Otherwise, the two tokens *definitely do not overlap*.

Assume we have a token representing *Miguel's sleep* in the night to come. Assuming further that the user knows that Miguel sleeps until 8:00, there is definitely no overlap with *Pedro's availability;* if it is known that Miguel sleeps until between 9:00 and 9:30, there is a definite overlap; and if all that is known is that he sleeps until between 8:00 and 9:30, there is a non-definite overlap.

Definition 7 (Token inconsistency) Two tokens are called *inconsistent* if they are contradictory and definitely or non-definitely overlapping.

4 Concepts for Dealing with (Vague) Temporal Information

Based on these notions, we will now describe some key concepts for general time map management as implemented in the MTMM. For a more detailed description, we refer to [Materne 90].

4.1 Persistence Clipping

There is a particular subproblem in time map management: what to do if a time map contains a token inconsistency? Intuitively, consider a fact f holding at some point p and another fact g holding at q; furthermore consider that f contradicts g and $p=q$. Something is wrong, then, but what to do?

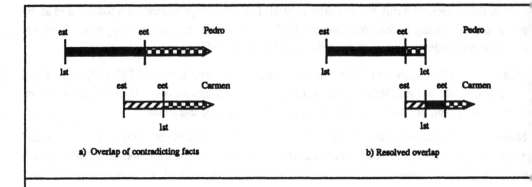

Figure 2 Persistence clipping in Example 1

The concept of *persistence clipping* allows to handle token inconsistencies, where the overlap of the tokens involved is *non-definite*. Note that trying to prevent a *definite* overlap by introducing further constraints would result in a constraint inconsistency, i.e., when there is a definite overlap of contradictory tokens, there is nothing simply to repair, but information given must be *withdrawn*, which is beyond the competence of time map management and is *no* case for persistence clipping.

In case of a non-definite overlap we will have to deal with the token start order. Defining this is a bit clumsy because we have to respect all possible combinations of the minimized relation between the token start points and the boundary types of the tokens; as the formal definition is mostly technical, we skip it here and refer to [Materne/Hertzberg/Voß 90]. Mind, however, that the start order of two tokens may be undetermined, e.g., if the minimized relation between the two respective start points is $<x,y>$, where $x<0$ and $y>0$.

On first sight, the idea is that the contradictory token starting later clips the persistence (i.e. the token interval) of the token starting earlier, resulting in a consistent time map. But this is not the whole story. Consider the following addendum to the basic example:

Example 1: Claudia tells that Carmen wants to go shopping tomorrow; she will arrive at the beach any time between 10:00 and 11:00.

The "hard" minimum availability of Pedro (i.e., the time until 10:30) constrains Carmen's arrival to the interval between 10:30 and 11:00; Carmen's seizing interval, on the other hand, constrains Pedro's availability to end between 10:30 and 11:00, too. *Both* intervals should be cut, not only the one starting earlier, cf. Figure 2.

Compared with Dean's ideas, persistence clipping is more general in three respects[2]:

- It is not *persistence* that is clipped, but *vagueness about persistence.*, e.g., vagueness of the persistence of *Pedro's availability.*

---

[2]Hence, the term *persistence clipping* is misleading. For historical reasons, we stick to it.

- Not only the token interval may be clipped, but also (vagueness of) possible start and end times, e.g., Carmen's arrival time.
- Not only the token starting before the other is clipped, but persistence clipping is symmetric wrt. the tokens involved: it may resolve in clipping the earlier or the later or both tokens.

These three general features of persistence clipping are different, independent *effects* of introducing and propagating the *uniform* clipping constraint $[0, \infty]$ between the end point of the token starting not later and the start point of the other token. Independently of what effects actually occur, the overlap is resolved.[3]

Different to Dean's TMM philosophy, it may make sense for a user to decide—at his risk—to postpone persistence clipping or not to clip at all, at the cost of an inconsistent time map. Consider, e.g., that Timm wants to record information in his time map that contradicts Miguel's availability in the afternoon. To be watertightly consistent, the persistence concerning the "Miguel token" would have to be clipped; on the other hand, Timm isn't interested in any boatman's availability after lunch and might consider it wasting energy to keep track of unimportant clipping information. It is up to him to decide which information is important and which is not; a time map management system would only be responsible for not using contradicted information, which is guaranteed in the MTMM by actually making no deductions.

Note that it makes no difference for determining the minimal relations in a time map whether you introduce a clipping constraint sooner or later: you may first work with a time map and then introduce a clipping constraint or the other way round; the minimized relations obtained in the end are equal. Like the uniqueness of the minimized relations, this result is due to the properties of local propagation in filtering constraint networks [Güsgen/Hertzberg 88], see also [Materne 90].

The point is: A user may have any sorts of reasons for not being interested in running a watertightly token consistent time map. If he would tolerate the risk concerning the information used, the system should allow him to do so. On the other hand, he should have the opportunity to ask the system to enforce consistency at any time later when he changes his mind. (Think, e.g., Timm decides to defer water skiing until the afternoon and needs the respective availabilities for that time.) See [Materne 90, Materne/Hertzberg/ Voß 90] for a more detailed discussion of this and persistence clipping in general.

4.2 Persistence and Validity

It is common in reasoning about dynamic worlds to assume that a fact persists as long as nothing to the contrary is known—see, e.g., the literature on the frame problem or extended prediction problem [Shoham/McDermott 88]. A time map manager should do so, too, and Dean's TMM in fact does. A system should, e.g., conclude in Example 1 that Pedro isn't

---

[3]Mind the tiny details, however! You must care for the boundary types of the two tokens involved in the obvious ways to prevent an overlap in the "clipping point". We skip this here for brevity.

available at, say, 12:30 (if the user has agreed to do clip persistence). In the basic example, however, it intuitively might conclude that he *is* available at that time.

This latter conclusion in the basic example is based on an additional, non-trivial assumption that we call the *basic rule of persistence* and that is implemented in the MTMM as follows:

Every token is assumed to persist for and no longer than the value of its upper bound.[4]

Again, this is a perfectly general rule neatly applicable to all possible special cases: it handles both exact and vague tokens and tokens with both a numeric upper bound and the upper bound ∞. In our basic example, Pedro is in fact considered available for ∞, and Miguel for 6 hours, if applying this rule. It implements an optimistic view concerning persistence[5]; on the other hand, it doesn't lead to "over-optimistic" conclusions: it forces you, e.g., to be agnostic about the availability of Miguel after the 6 hours even if nothing is known to the contrary, just because this is the upper bound of the respective token interval.

Now, recall that Timm's question in our example is which boatman is available for 1 to 1.5 hours between 10:30 and 1:00. Intuitively, he runs a risk if hiring Pedro because Pedro may be off with Carmen after 10:30. The basic rule of persistence, on the other hand, says that Pedro's availability persists for ∞.

What should we make out of this conflict? It is *no* answer to say that the basic rule of persistence is simply wrong. Its conclusion, e.g., concerning Pedro's availability may exactly be what Timm wants. (Pedro is cheaper, and Timm is willing to accept some risk at the reward of being hauled by him.) The point is that there isn't *the* rule of persistence, but it depends on pragmatic circumstances, what you are willing to accept as true—or as *sufficiently grounded* (or *valid,* for short), to avoid the term *true* which is misleading because it suggests a false generality.

A time map management system should not include just a *single* rule of persistence or a *single* predicate to determine the validity of a fact over the points in a given interval like TMM's [Dean/McDermott 87] *true-throughout* predicate; *two true-throughout* predicates as in [Dean/Boddy 87] are no solution either.[6] There are a whole number of mutually independent features of a validity predicate; a time map management system should offer a whole family of these predicates or even a "validity predicate construction set". The question to answer, in general, is, sloppily stated: given two points P_1, P_2 and a token type T, find a token t of type T that is valid over the interval I between P_1 and P_2. Features to observe when defining a validity predicate are, e.g.,

- the token interval,
- the duration of the interval I,

---

[4]Note that Dean *uses* this basic rule of persistence [Dean/McDermott 87]. However what he *calls* rule of persistence in fact models what we call persistence clipping. In fact, he uses the term "rule of persistence" in a similar sense to persistence clipping.

[5]Note that we are optimistic about the *persistence* of a token, not its content. There may be people considering it *pessimistic* to assume maximal persistence of *My car is broken;* but that is a different thing.

[6]Note that Dean [Dean/McDermott 87] treats the rule of persistence and the validity predicate as more or less independent. As they are two sides of the same medal, we discuss them in common.

- the relation between the reference point and the start of *I*,
- the relation between the reference point and the start of the token,
- the relation between the reference point and the end of *I*, and
- the relation between the reference point and the end of the token.

All these features may be vague, and for all of these you have to decide whether to consider the smallest or the greatest value or any value in between. Let us see two examples:

- Timm is interested in being able to fix his water skiing definitely, independent from his physical condition tomorrow; i.e., the availability token interval must definitely span the maximal water skiing duration of 1.5 hours, at least, within the interval between his earliest water skiing start at 10:30 and his latest end at 1:00. This leaves Miguel as the only solution.
- Timm is interested in starting earliest possible; i.e., the availability token must definitely start at or before 10:30 and possibly persist until 11:30, at least. This leaves Pedro as the only solution (with the bit of risk that his availability may end before 11:30).

To sum up, different combinations of validity features lead to different answers as to which boatmen possibly to hire, and most of them are arguable. There is no unique notion of validity in MTMM's time maps, and what is regarded as valid depends on the validity predicate used. It is up to the user of the MTMM to choose a convenient validity predicate, i.e., the combination of validity features that is appropriate for the problem domain at hand.

5   MTMM Features

The general concepts and definitions are implemented in the MTMM as described. As a summary, we will briefly state some key issues we gain from building on the theory presented in section 3. All this is discussed in more detail in [Materne 90].

A time map managed by the MTMM is constraint consistent. The essence of the proof of this claim is that (1) it is possible to detect every constraint inconsistency as soon as the user inputs a constraint and that (2) the user is forced to avoid it.

A time map managed by the MTMM is "complete", where completeness means using *all* information contained in the time map. As there is no generally accepted time map management semantics, all one can do is making that claim plausible; this is done in [Materne 90].

The user of the MTMM is allowed to withdraw any information given at any time, so the user may run what-if experiments. This is a result of excessively using reason maintenance, or a slight modification of a Doyle-style TMS [Doyle 1979], to be precise. Obviously, you must pay for the desire for flexibility with computation time.

The MTMM can handle purely qualitative *temporal models.* The essence of time map management is dealing with *quantitative* temporal information. In some applications, however, we have to deal with mere *qualitative* temporal information (namely, *before, equal, after,* and disjunctive combinations of these). MTMM can handle these abstractions consistently and completely by translating them internally into quantitative ones (e.g., *before* is treated as $[1,\infty]$) and re-translating the quantitative results. Note, however, that it is not always possible to mix up a quantitatively and a qualitatively interpreted time map without running the risk of obtaining unintuitive results.

MTMM's qualitative models are a practically relevant subset of Allen's [83] temporal logics. Obviously, dealing with *quantitative* temporal information is beyond the scope of Allen's logics. When, however, interpreting MTMM's temporal relations *qualitatively*, we arrive at a proper subset of the Allen relations: the *convex* relations, as they are called by Nökel [89]. Nökel [89] shows, however, that the convex relations allow nearly all practical problems to be formalized. Different to Allen's logics, convex relations (i.e., both Nökel's and MTMM's) can*not* express that some interval is *before or after* (but not overlapping) another.[7]

On the other hand, the point-basedness of the MTMM allows some problems to be formalized in a more intuitive way than is possible in Allen's logics: think of Allen and Hayes's [87] example of throwing a ball.

The MTMM is implemented in Allegro Common Lisp on the Apple Macintosh.

References

[Allen 83]: Allen, J.F.: Maintaining Knowledge about Temporal Intervals. C.acm, *26* (1983), 832

[Allen/Hayes 87]: Allen, J.F./ Hayes, P.: Short Time Periods. Proc. IJCAI-87, 981

[Dean 85]: Dean, T.L.: Temporal imagery: An approach to reasoning about time for planning and problem solving. Tech. Report 433, Comp. Sci. Dept., Yale Univ., New Haven CT, 1985

[Dean/Boddy 87]: Dean, T.L./ Boddy, M.: Incremental Causal Reasoning. Proc. AAAI-87, 196

[Dean/McDermott 87]: Dean, T.L./ McDermott, D.V.: Temporal Data Base Management. J. Art. Int., *32* (1987), 1

[Doyle 1979]: Doyle, J.: A Truth Maintenance System. Art. Int, *12* (1979), 231

[Drabble 88]: Drabble, B.: Planning and Reasoning with Processes. AIAI-TR-56, Artificial Intelligence Applications Institute, Univ. of Edinburgh, Nov. 1988

[Fikes/Nilsson 71]: Fikes, R.E./ Nilsson, N.J.: STRIPS: A New Approach to the Application of Theorem Proving to Problem Solving. Art. Int., *2*, 189 (1971)

[Forbus 84]: Forbus, K.D.: Qualitative Process Theory. J. Art. Int., *24* (1984), 85

[Ginsberg/Smith 88]: Ginsberg, M.L./ Smith, D.E.: Reasoning About Action I: A Possible Worlds Approach. J. Art. Int., *35* (1988), 165

[Güsgen/Hertzberg 88]: Güsgen, H.W./ Hertzberg, J.: Some Fundamental Properties of Local Constraint Propagation. in: J. Artificial Intelligence, *36*, 237 (1988)

[Hanks/McDermott 85]: Hanks, S./ McDermott D.: Temporal Reasoning and Default Logics. YALEU/CSD/RR#430, Yale Univ., Dept. of Computer Science, Oct 1985

---

[7]Well, using a trick (involving contradicting token types), you can even express mutual exclusion in the MTMM, which is beyond Nökel's convex relations.

[deKleer/Brown 84]: deKleer, J./ Brown, J.S.: A Qualitative Physics Based on Confluences. J. Art. Int., *24* (1984), 7

[Materne 90]: Materne, S.: MTMM – Ein System zur Verwaltung von Zeitverhältnissen. Diploma Thesis, Computer Science Dept., Bonn University, June 1990 (in German). To be published as GMD-Bericht, München (Oldenbourg Verlag) 1991

[Materne/Hertzberg/Voß 90]: Materne, S./ Hertzberg, J./ Voß, H.: On Clipping Persistence (Or Whatever Must Be Clipped) in Time Maps. Submitted paper.

[McCarthy/Hayes 69]: McCarthy, J./ Hayes, P.J.: Some Philosophical Problems from the Standpoint of Artificial Intelligence. Mach. Int., *4* (1969)

[Nökel 89]: Nökel, K.: Convex Relations Between Time Intervals. Proc. ÖGAI-89, (Berlin (Springer) 1989), 298

[Shoham/McDermott 88]: Shoham, Y./ McDermott, D.V.: Problems in Formal Temporal Reasoning. Art. Int., *36* (1988), 49

[Vere 83]: Vere, S.A.: Planning in Time: Windows and Durations for Activities and Goals. IEEE Trans. *PAMI-5,* 246 (1983)

[Voß/Linster 89]: Voß, H./ Linster, M.: Interval-based Envisioning in HIQUAL. Applied Art. Int., *3* (1989), 17

COMPLETE DETERMINATION OF PARALLEL ACTIONS AND TEMPORAL OPTIMIZATION IN LINEAR PLANS OF ACTION

Pierre REGNIER   Bernard FADE

Equipe IA et Robotique, IRIT, Université Paul Sabatier
118 rte. de Narbonne, 31062 Toulouse cedex
Tel: 61.55.66.11 (72.63), E-mail: regnier@irit.fr

Abstract: Traditional non-linear planners (NOAH, NONLIN, SIPE, ...) construct plans of actions by progressively introducing and partially ordering actions in the initial plan to satisfy a set of constraints. On the other hand, our method, using the triangle table formalism, enables the planner to easily determine, in linear (over constrained) plans, all actions which can be executed in parallel (removing from the linear plan all the artificial order constraints). This information may then be used by a classical algorithm to optimize the resulting plan's execution time.

Keywords: Linear plans of action, non-linear planning, parallel actions, triangle table, temporal optimization.

1-INTRODUCTION: In a previous paper (cf. [FAD-89], [REG-90.a] § 8 and 9) a complete method for the determination of parallelism of contiguous groups of actions in linear plans has been presented. After a brief overview of planning and a short review of our method, we will show how to determine the complete set of actions which can be executed in parallel. We shall then explain how this information may be used to optimize the resulting plan's execution time.

2-OVERVIEW OF PLANNING: A planner is a knowledge based system; it takes as input a description of the initial world state, a description of goals to achieve, a description of actions that can be taken in the world and generates a sequence of actions (or plan) which can be executed to transform the initial world state into a state that achieves the given goals (cf. [HEN-90], [REG-90.b] for state of the art). Depending on the system, the generated plan's structure may be quite different: linear plans or non-linear plans may be built.

2.1-Linear and non-linear plans: A linear plan is a plan produced by a linear planner: in these plans, actions are totally ordered. These plans are over-constrained: the fact that a sequential ordering of the actions is imposed by the planning process adds "artificial" order constraints to the "genuine" constraints due to the fact that one action is prerequisite to another.

Example: A_1: Pick up the screwdriver;
A_2: Pick up the screw;
A_3: Place the screw in the hole;
A_4: Place the screwdriver in the screw;
A_5: Turn the screwdriver.

A non-linear plan is a plan produced by a non-linear planner. These plans contain only necessary (genuine) constraints: if there is no reason to place one action before another then the two actions are not ordered. The planning process does not add artificial order constraints to the plan. Because such a plan does not contain unnecessary contraints, we will call it a well-constrained plan; if the set of constraint is not too strong, the plan can remain partially ordered: it contains actions which can be executed concurrently. In the following example, S is a split node and J a join node:

Example:
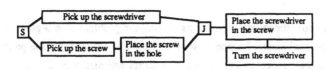

Remark: The principal use of a partially ordered plan is to optimize the execution time by taking advantage of the agent's executing capabilities for parallel actions. If the agent who executes the plan does not have the means to execute parallel actions, this plan must be linearised before execution. For example, the above plan's execution by a person who can only use a single hand. In this case, another advantage of a partially ordered plan is that one can choose the execution order of actions at the last moment.

2.2-Non-linear planning: So far, the only planners which can produce partially ordered plans are non-linear planners of NOAH's family [SAC-74], [SAC-75.a/b] (criteria for evaluating these planners may be found in [KAR-90]). The non-linear planning strategy (also called least commitment strategy) used by these planners consists of reducing problems to a (a priori non ordered) set of sub-problems and progressively detecting and then resolving interactions between them in order to have as few constraints as possible in the produced plan. Using this strategy, the resulting plans of action can be (depending on the set of constraints) partially ordered since actions which do not interact can be executed concurrently. Sacerdoti used this approach for the first time in NOAH [SAC-74], [SAC-75.a/b], Tate with his system NONLIN [TAT-77] then Wilkins in SIPE [WIL-83], [WIL-84], [WIL-88] improved it. More recently, Chapman, with his planner TWEAK [CHA-87] has done important theoretical work on non-linear planning.

In NOAH, the current plan is stored in a procedural net and goal interactions are detected by means of a TOME (Table Of Multiple Effects) which contains the global word changes relative to each node. Programs called Critics search the TOME for actions (or operators) with contradictory effects and then resolve interactions by properly ordering the actions concerned or by the addition of new actions to the plan. Thus, the final plan is built by a progressive partial linearization of an initial plan so as to satisfy a set of constraints. Furthermore, all the NOAH's family planners closely associate the least commitment strategy and an operator hierarchy to prevent the combinatorial explosion that would result from a direct application of the constraint set (the plan is developed progressively at different levels of detail). NOAH only uses an operator hierarchy, Wilkins, in SIPE, improves it by using a hierarchical description of the invariable world (frame representation).

Remark: The expression "non-linear planning" is often understood as a process whose result is the production of partially ordered plans. This interpretation is only partially correct: in fact, the word non-linear refers to the giving up of the linearity assumption employed in HACKER's [SUS-73] family planners (WARPLAN [WAR-74], Waldinger's system [WAL-77], ...). In these planners one tries to solve sub-problems in an *a priori* given order which is corrected to take into account interactions between them. The achievement of partially ordered plans is only a result of the non-linear planning strategy which can moreover produce totally ordered plans if the set of constraints is strong enough.

If the use of least commitment strategy allows solving the problem of sub-goals interaction and may produce partially ordered plans of action, it would be naïve to suppose it is the panacea of all planning problems. Here are some reflections about the advantages and disadvantadges of linear and non-linear planning to justify our method.

2.3-The reasoning behind our method:

1-Only certain problems relative to specific fields absolutely require non-linear planning for their resolution, in many fields, linear planning is sufficient to solve the given problem. In these fields, a partially ordered plan is merely an optimisation (with respect to execution time) of the linear version.

2-In most cases, the order for the resolution of sub-goals is part of the domain's knowledge (when one knows the set of sub-problems to be solved to achieve a given goal, one often knows the order necessary for their solution). Traditional non-linear planners (NOAH, NONLIN, SIPE, ...) do not directly take this fact into account; that is why, doing a partial linearization of the initial plan, they perform many tasks which a different formalism or a better representation of knowledge could eliminate (see [IRA-87] and [CHE-89] for recent works about this problem).

3-Contrary to linear planners (BUILD [FAH-74], SRI system [FIK-75], Waldinger's system [WAL-77], ...), non-linear planners cannot be used to rigourously extend the STRIPS representation of actions and take into account side effects and context dependent effects of actions (on this subject, cf. [WAL-77], [CHA-87], [WIL-88], [GIN-88]). With these planners, only narrow fields can be represented.

4-Non-linear planners are often hierarchical whereas the possibility of parallelism is situated at the level of primitive actions (directly executable) rather than higher up in the plan structure (non-executable operators). These planners strongly associate parallelism and hierarchy [WIL-86] but the operator's hierarchical structure is only an artificial method of progressively introducing constraints in the plan so as to prevent the combinatorial explosion that would result from the direct application of the complete set of constraint. Only Wilkins, with SIPE, tries to connect the plan's hierarchical structure to a partial hierarchical description of the world.

5-In non-linear planners, the truth criterion (procedure for determining the truth value of a fact at any step of the planning process) is rather expensive (because of its complexity [CHA-87], [WIL-88]); in linear planners, this procedure is straightforward.

6-Non-linear planning allows solving the problem of sub-goals interactions, linear planning methods [SUS-73], [WAR-74], [TAT-77], [WAL-77], if they are often efficient, are less general.

7-Only non-linear planning has been proven to be a complete process (with the qualification of a STRIPS representation of actions).

Taking into consideration the preceding remarks, we have developed the following method: linear and hierarchical planning by means of an object oriented representation (hierarchical production of the plan connected to hierarchical representation of the world). Then, search for all actions which may be executed in parallel (mapping from an over-constrained, totally ordered plan to a well-constrained and possibly less ordered plan) and use of this information to optimize the resulting plan's execution time. In our planner, side effects of actions can also be represented. In this paper we will deal only with search for parallelism and temporal optimization of the plan; for this, we will use a simple representation of knowledge.

3-A CLASSICAL REPRESENTATION OF THE WORD:

3.1-Use of STRIPS's formalism: In our planner we use STRIPS's formalism (from the name of the first planner which used this pattern, cf. [FIK-71.a/b], [FIK-72.a/b] and also [LIF-86] for a study of STRIPS's semantic); in accordance with STRIPS's representation, actions are of the type:

(<Name-of-the-action (arguments) ><Preconditions><Add-list><Delete-list>)

Where: -Preconditions: List of necessary conditions for the execution of the action.

-Add-list: List of facts added to the world description when the action is executed.

-Delete-list: List of facts removed from the world description when the action is executed.

For simplicity, we group together the Add and Delete lists in a single one called Effects. Facts which are removed are marked with the ¬ symbol (literals of this form are called <u>negative literals</u>, others are <u>positive literals</u>). The Preconditions and Effects lists contain literals of the following form (predicate logic representation and infix notation):

(<Object><Attribute><Value>)

Where: -Attribute is a two place predicate symbol.

-Object and Value are its arguments.

Example: PICKUP action in a block-world.

> **PICKUP ?x**
> Preconditions: (?x ON ?y)(?x Covered_By nil)(hand State empty)
> Effects: (?x IN hand)(hand State full)(?y Covered_By nil)¬(?x ON ?y)
> ¬(?x Covered_By nil)¬(hand State empty)¬(?y Covered_By ?x)

3.2-Non-contradictory literals: A pair of literals is defined to be <u>contradictory</u> if it is in one of the following forms (all others pairs are defined to be <u>Non-Contradictory</u>).

(Object_1 Attribute_1 Value_1)   (Object_1 Attribute_1 Value_2) where Value_1 ≠ Value_2

(Object_1 Attribute_1 Value_1)   ¬(Object_1 Attribute_1 Value_1)

A <u>global world state</u> is defined by a set (an implicit conjunction) of non-contradictory positive literals. When the union of two sets of literals does not contain contradictory pairs, these sets are said to be <u>compatible</u>. We also require the <u>closed world hypothesis</u>: the truth value of literals which are not members of the description of the world state is False (all others have the truth value True).

3.3-The discrete assumption: When they are performed, actions represent an <u>instantaneous change</u> of world state. Even if the execution of an action needs a certain time lapse (*a priori* unknown), <u>preconditions must be true during all the execution time. At the end of this execution, effects are instantaneous and preconditions can be modified</u>. Even so, a composition of discrete actions can represent actions whose effects progressively appear or whose preconditions disappear with time (for example, cf. [VER-81]).

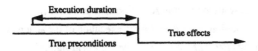

We will now study the necessary and sufficient conditions for the parallel execution of two actions in a linear plan.

4-NECESSARY AND SUFFICIENT CONDITIONS PERMITTING THE PARALLEL EXECUTION OF TWO ACTIONS IN A LINEAR PLAN:

Two actions are said to be executable in parallel if and only if (iff) they *may be executed in any order* and if the intersection of their intervals of execution may be arbitrary (there is no temporal dependence between them). Note that the lack of ordering between two actions does not *require* that they co-occur; the co-occurence is only *permitted* (cf. [GRO-91] in these proceedings for a formalization of actions that must co-occur).

4.1-The conditions: Let (A_i Preconditions_i Effects_i) and (A_j Preconditions_j Effects_j) be two actions of a linear plan (i<j), described according to the hypothesis of § 3.1 and 3.3. A_i and A_j can be executed in parallel iff the following five conditions are simultaneously satisfied (cf. [REG-90.a] § 6):

    1-The sets Preconditions_i, Preconditions_j are compatible and included in the world state preceding the execution of A_i and A_j.
    2-The sets Effects_i and Effects_j are compatible.
    3-The sets Preconditions_i and Effects_j are compatible.
    4-The sets Effects_i and Preconditions_j are compatible.
    5-There is not any sequence of actions (A_i, ..., A_n, ..., A_j) (i<n<j) such that every couple of successive actions in this sequence should not be executed in parallel.

A part of our method for searching for parallelism is based on the fact that when the two actions A_i and A_j are members of a linear plan memorised in a <u>Triangle Table</u> (TT), it is possible to reduce the number of conditions to three (note that the triangle table is not absolutely necessary, any plan teleological structure is sufficient). We will now briefly study the structure of this table before exposing the method for the determination of parallel actions.

4.2-Using the triangle table: The triangle table is a particular representation for linear plans of action. It was originally developed by Fikes, Hart, Nilsson and Munson to control the execution of plans produced by their STRIPS planner [FIK-71.a/b], [FIK-72.a/b]. It has also been shown to have many others applications [FIK-72.b], [NIL-85], [PIC-87].

No method among the classical ones [FIK-71.a/b], [PIC-87] constructs the TT in a manner suitable for the extraction of parallel actions (redundancy of literals, abscence of certain effects, ...). So, we have developed another method which is suitable. The table is incrementally constructed during the planning phase (allowing its use for backtracking during simulation and for solving subgoals interactions, cf. [REG-90.a]). The following is a description of the triangle table that we generate:

-The plan follows the diagonal from top (action A_1) to bottom (action A_d).
-Each row i contains all the conditions necessary for the execution of the action A_i.
-*Each column i contains all the effects of the action A_i on the world state.*
-The first column contains the initially existant conditions necessary for the execution of the plan.
-The last row (at the bottom) contains the terminal effects (facts added) of the plan.
-The preconditions and effects of the actions in the plan are positioned in the table as a result of their use by the various actions.
-*The only redundancies of literals tolerated are those which are strictly necessary.*

Simple example in a block-world:

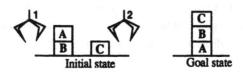

Initial state   Goal state

Model of actions in the block-world (?x and ?y are variables):

    PICKUP ?x
        Preconditions: (?x ON ?y)(?x Covered_By nil)(hand State empty)
        Effects: (?x IN hand)(hand State full)(?y Covered_By nil)¬(?x ON ?y)
                 ¬(?x Covered_By nil)¬(hand State empty)¬(?y Covered_By ?x)

    PUT_ON ?x ?y
        Preconditions: (?y Covered_By nil)(?x IN hand)(hand State full)
        Effects: (?x ON ?y)(?x Covered_By nil)(hand State empty)(?y Covered_By ?x)
                 ¬(?y Covered_By nil)¬(?x IN hand)¬(hand State full)

Triangle table representing the plan which solves this problem:

	0	1	2	3	4	5	6
1	(A On B) (A CB nil) (hand1Sempty)	1_PICKUP A					
2	(table S free)	(hand1Sfull) (A IN hand1)	1_PUT_ON A table				
3	(B ON table) (hand2Sempty)	(B CB nil)		2_PICKUP B			
4			(A CB nil)	(hand2Sfull) (BINhand2)	2_PUT_ON B A		
5	(C ON table) (C CB nil)		(hand1Sempty)			1_PICK_UP C	
6					(B CB nil)	(hand1Sfull) (C IN hand1)	1_PUT_ON C B
7			(A ON table)		(A CB B) (B ON A) (hand2Sempty)		(B CB C)(C ON B) (C CB nil) (hand1Sempty)

4.3-New conditions for the parallel execution of two actions in a TT: Using the TT, it is possible to reduce to three the number of conditions which two actions of a linear plan must meet so as to be executable in parallel (the following theorems have been proven in [REG-90.a]):

Theorem: Two actions A_i and A_j ($i<j$) of a linear plan stored in a TT can be executed in parallel iff the following three conditions are simultaneously satisfied:

1-The cell $C_{i,j}$ is empty.

2-Preconditions_i and Effects_j are compatible sets (in fact, the subset of preconditions which are not modified by Ai is sufficient).

3-There is not any sequence of actions $(A_i, ..., A_n, ..., A_j)$ ($i<n<j$) such that every couple of successive actions in this sequence should not be executed in parallel.

Even if this theorem can be directly used to determine an important subset of actions which can be executed in parallel (condition 3 is automatically satisfied by actions which are part of parallel contiguous groups of actions, cf. [REG-90.a] § 8), the < relation is required to easily determine all the parallel actions. This relation, as we will see, is complementary to the parallelism relation.

5-ORDER OF TWO ACTIONS AND USE OF THE GRAPH REPRESENTATION:

5.1-Definition of the order of two actions: Two actions A_i and A_j ($i<j$) in a linear plan are said to be ordered (and we will write $A_i<A_j$) iff these two actions cannot be executed in parallel. So, A_i and A_j will be ordered iff one of the following three conditions is satisfied:

1-The cell $C_{i,j}$ is not empty.

2-Preconditions_i and Effects_j are incompatible sets (see remark in previous theorem).

3-There is at least one sequence of actions $(A_i, ..., A_n, ..., A_j)$ ($i<n<j$) such that every couple of successive actions in this sequence should be ordered (transitive relation).

The < relation is a strict order relation (non reflexive, anti-symmetrical, transitive). Usually, it is also a partial relation (in a plan, there are generally some actions which may be executed in parallel). The parallelism relation is non reflexive, symmetrical and non transitive. These two relations are complementary: the knowledge of one is sufficient to determine the other (they are not reflexive: only distinct actions are in the relations).

5.2-The graph representation: A graph representation can be used to represent order constraints between actions. These graphs are directed acyclic 1-graphs which may be characterized as follows (cf. potential-tasks graphs [ROY-60]):

-Each action is represented by a node labelled with the number of the action in the linear plan.

-When two actions A_i and A_j ($i<j$) must be ordered (A_i before A_j), there exists an arc (A_i, A_j) linking the corresponding nodes in the graph representation.

In most cases, a linear plan is never completely constrained (< is a strict partial order relation because some actions may be executed in parallel). The directed acyclic 1-graph representing the < relation will be called a Partially Ordered Graph (POG).

Example: If the < relation is defined by the set: {(1, 6), (1, 7), (2, 4), (2, 5), (2, 6), (2, 7), (3, 4), (3, 5), (3, 6), (3, 7), (4, 5), (4, 6), (4, 7)}, we will have the following POG:

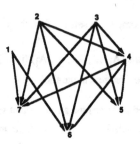

5.3-Algorithm for the construction of the POG from the TT: The most efficient means for this construction is to use the triangle table for the determination of couples of actions which must be ordered. For this, we employ < as defined above; the cells of the TT are incrementally examined, from top to bottom and from right to left; every full cell $C_{i,j}$ or cell for which Preconditions_i and Effects_j are incompatible sets denotes two ordered actions A_i and A_j (we shall indicate these couples of ordered actions by (A_i, A_j)). The transitivity of the < relation is taken into account by the **Transitivity** function as soon as ordered couples of actions are added.

```
POG (TT);

Begin
    POG <- {};
    tt_size <- size (TT);
    current_cell <- (1, 2);
    While ≤ (ordinate (current_cell), tt_size) Do
        While ≥ (abscissa (current_cell), 1) Do
            If not (parallelism (current_cell, TT))
            Then POG <- transitivity (POG, current_cell);
            current_cell <- (abscissa (current_cell) - 1, ordinate (current_cell));
        End;
        current_cell <- (ordinate (current_cell), ordinate (current_cell) + 1);
    End;
End.
```

Size: this function returns the size (number of actions) of the TT it receives as argument.

Abscissa: (resp. **ordonate**) this function returns the abscissa (resp. ordonate) of the cell it receives as argument (column number, resp. row number) .

Parallelism: using as argument a cell $C_{i,j}$, this predicate returns true if the cell is empty or if the sets Preconditions_i and Effects_j are compatible, false otherwise.

Not, Equal, >, ≥, <, ≤: usual definitions.

5.4-The complete determination of the parallel pairs of actions: Since the parallelism relation is complementary to <, the pairs of actions which are not mutually constrained are the set of parallel actions. For example, the previous POG produces the parallel_set = {(1, 2), (1, 3), (1, 4), (1, 5), (2, 3), (5, 6), (5, 7), (6, 7)} and the § 4.2 block-world example produces parallel_set = {(2, 3), (3, 5), (4, 5)}.

6-TEMPORAL OPTIMIZATION OF LINEAR PLANS OF ACTION: Using the POG and a classical graph processing algorithm, it is easy to solve the problem of action execution order to obtain the minimal execution time of the plan.

6.1-The algorithm for temporal optimization: Our method is based on a classical algorithm for searching for nodes without predecessors (it will not be describe here because it is a very classical one). If a pair of actions (A_i, A_j) satisfies the < relation, then it is impossible to execute A_j before the termination of A_i. Since we have a POG which represents order constraints between the various actions, a search for nodes which depend on no other will produce the set of actions which may be executed concurrently. As soon as the execution of one of these actions is terminated, the POG is modified: the node representing the executed action is erased with all arcs originating there. A new search for nodes without predecessors produces the new set of executable actions. This process must be dynamic and finishes when all the actions in the plan have been executed. One of the advantages of this method (beyond the simplicity) is that the temporal optimization of the plan does not require knowledge about each action's execution time :

1-An action is executed as soon as it appears in the set of executable actions.

2-The termination of an action liberates all those which only depend upon it: they then become executable.

Remark-1: If one knows in advance the execution time of all the actions, then all the classical graph theory methods may be used (potential-tasks graphs [ROY-60], PERT graphs [MAL-59], ...) to determine the plan's minimal execution time, actions which must be successful to obtain it, ...

Remark-2: For temporal optimization, it is not necessary to construct a complete POG: a POG without transitive closure is sufficient.

6.2-Example: The POG corresponding to the parallel_set {(1, 2), (1, 3), (1, 4), (1, 5), (2, 3), (5, 6), (5, 7), (6, 7)} from the example of § 5.2 is:

The set of actions which may be executed is: executable_set = {1, 2, 3}. These actions may therefore be executed in parallel. Once these actions have all terminated, a search in the updated graph produces executable_set = {4} :

After termination of action 4, the set_of_executable_actions will be {5, 6, 7}, and these actions may be executed in parallel.

Remark: It is not necessary to wait for the termination of all actions in the executable_set to begin a new search. The set of executable actions may have changed if only one of these is terminated. For example, if actions 2 and 3 terminate before action 1, one can execute action 4, then action 5.

7_CONCLUSION: We have proposed a method for the determination of parallelism in a linear plan. Once determined, this parallelism may be used, with the help of classical algorithms, to optimize the plan's execution time (cf. the above method), to determine the maximal sets of parallel actions (cf. [REG-90.a] § 12), to determine the minimal execution time of the plan and actions which must be successful to obtain it (cf. [ROY-60], [MAL-59]). Certain difficult aspects of our method have not been presented here (contents of the TT, reduction of the number of parallelism conditions, ...); for the latter of these, one may refer to [REG-90.a]. All of the algorithms presented have been implemented and fully tested in Lisp. Although parallelism is the center of our research, the conception of our planner has raised many other issues. In particular, we are defining a linear and hierarchical planning process by means of an object oriented representation (hierarchical production of the plan connected to hierarchical representation of the world).

8-BIBLIOGRAPHY:

CHA-87 D.Chapman, "Planning for conjunctive goals", Artificial intelligence, n°32, 1987.

CHE-89 J.Cheng, K.B.Irani, "Ordering problem sub-goals", IJCAI, 1989.

FAD-89 B.Fade, P.Regnier, "Une méthode complète de recherche du parallélisme dans les plans d'actions linéaires", Congrés AFCET-RFIA, Paris, 1989.

FAH-74 S.E.Falhman, "A planning system for robot construction tasks", Artificial intelligence n° 1, 1974.

FIK-71.a R.E.Fikes, N.J.Nilsson, "STRIPS: a new approach to the application of theorem proving to problem solving", Artificial intelligence n°2, 1971.

FIK-71.b R.E.Fikes, "Monitored execution of robot plan produced by STRIPS", IFIP, Yugoslavia, 1971.

FIK-72.a R.E.Fikes, P.E.Hart, N.J.Nilsson, "Some new directions in robot problem solving", Machine intelligence n°7, 1972.

FIK-72.b R.E.Fikes, P.E.Hart, N.J.Nilsson, "Learning and executing generalized robot plans", Artificial intelligence n°3, 1972.

FIK-75 R.E.Fikes, "Deductive retrievial mechanisms for state description models", Technical note n° 106, AI center, SRI, 1975.

GIN-88 M.L.Ginsberg, D.E.Smith, "Reasoning about actions 1: a possible worlds approch", "Reasoning about actions 2: the qualification problem", Artificial intelligence n°35, 1988.

GRO-91 G.Große, R.Waldinger, "Toward a theory of simultaneous actions", First European workshop on planning, EWSP, 1991 (à paraitre).

HEN-90 J.Hendler, A.Tate, M.Drummond, "AI planning: systems and techniques", AAAI, 1990.

IRA-87 K.B.Irani, J.Cheng, "Sub-goal ordering and goal augmentation for heuristic problem solving", IJCAI, 1987.

KAR-90 N.A.Kartam, E.D.Wilkins, "Towards a foundation for evaluating AI planners", AI EDAM, Academic press, n°1, Vol.4, 1990.

LIF-86 V.Lifschitz, "On the semantics of STRIPS", Proceedings of the 1986 workshop about actions and plans, 1986.

MAL-59 D.G.Malcolm & Col., "Application of a technique for research and development program evaluation", Operations research, Vol.7, n°5, 1959.

NIL-85 N.J.Nilsson, "Triangle tables: a proposal for a robot programming language", Technical note n°347, SRI International, February 1985.

PIC-87 J.F.Picardat, "Contrôle d'exécution, compréhension et apprentissage de plans d'actions: développement de la méthode de la table triangulaire", Thèse, IRIT, LSI, UPS-Toulouse, Juin 1987.

REG-90.a P.Regnier, "Optimisation temporelle des plans d'actions linéaires: une politique basée sur une méthode complète de recherche du parallélisme", Rapport IRIT n°90/9/R, IRIT, UPS-Toulouse, Février 1990.

REG-90.b P.Regnier, "Planification: historique, principes, problèmes et méthodes (de GPS à TWEAK)", Rapport IRIT n°90/22/R, IRIT, UPS-Toulouse, Juin 1990.

ROY-60 B.Roy, "Contribution de la théorie des graphes à l'étude des problèmes d'ordonnancement", Actes de la 2ème conférence internationale sur la recherche opérationnelle, Aix-en-Provence, 1960.

SAC-74 E.D.Sacerdoti, "Planning in a hierarchy of abstraction spaces", Artificial intelligence n°5, 1974.

SAC-75.a E.D.Sacerdoti, "The non linear nature of plans", IJCAI, 1975.

SAC-75.b E.D.Sacerdoti, "A structure for plans and behavior", Technical note n°109, Stanford research institute, AI center, 1975.

SUS-73 G.J.Sussman, "A computer model of skill acquisition", MIT, Artificial intelligence laboratory, Cambridge, Report AI-TR-297, 1973. (Massachusetts Institute of Technology, American Elsevier Publishing Company, 1975).

TAT-77 A.Tate, "Generating project networks", IJCAI, 1977.

VER-81 S.A.Vere, "Planning in time: windows and durations for activities and goals", Research report, Jet Propulsion Laboratory, Pasadena, 1981 (IEEE 1983).

WAL-77 R.Waldinger, "Achieving several goals simultaneously", Machine Intelligence, pp. 80-136, Elcock & Michie/Ellis Horwood, Eds., Chichester, Sussex, 1977.

WAR-74 D.H.D.Warren, "Warplan: a system for generating plans", Computational logic Dpt., Edinburgh, 1974.

WIL-83 D.E.Wilkins, "Representation in a domain independent planner", IJCAI, 1983.

WIL-84 D.E.Wilkins, "Domain-independent planning: representation and plan generation", Artificial intelligence n°22, April 1984.

WIL-86 D.E.Wilkins, "Hierarchical planning: definition, implementation", ECAI, 1986.

WIL-88 D.E.Wilkins, "Practical planning: extending the classical AI planning paradigm", Morgan Kaufmann Publishers, San Mateo, California, 1988.

Knowledge subgoals in plans

Sam Steel
Dept Computer Science, University of Essex
Colchester CO4 3SQ, UK
sam@uk.ac.essex

Abstract: Plans naturally contain subgoals about how the world must be. They arise as preconditions of actions in the plan - having keys in order to unlock doors and so on. Plans also contain subgoals about what the agent must know - combinations of safes, Mary's phone number, which way the outlaw went. Merely stipulating that actions and operands must be known is a hack. This paper offers an account of actions done under uncertainty. If the account is accepted, knowledge subgoals arise automatically, since plans done under uncertainty must still be adequate descriptions of what to do. Plans with knowledge subgoals turn out to be very like ordinary plans.

One of the standard ideas in AI planning is that actions are in plans so that their effects can achieve some goal in the plan - either a final goal, or the precondition of a later action. Let me start by labouring the point about the distinction between world preconditions and knowledge subgoals.

John wants to open a door. Why does he fetch the key? So that he holds it. That is a subgoal, because if John does the action of unlocking the door, and he is holding the key, then the door will be open.

But suppose John wants to open the safe. Why does he look at the piece of paper on which the combination of the safe is written? So that he knows the combination. That is a subgoal, because if John dials a number on the safe's lock, and the number is the combination of the safe, then the safe will be open.

I have laid those cases out as parallel as possible, so that the profound difference shows up. Both cases are, I submit, perfectly sensible stories. But in the first the effect of the earlier action ("John holds the key") really is the precondition of the later. In the second, the effect is "John knows the combination" and the precondition is "the number dialled is the combination of the safe". They are utterly different.

Some people try and avoid this by re-analyzing the action of opening the safe, so that it has the precondition (among others) that "Agent knows the combination of the safe". But I submit that this is rubbish. Suppose a bored chimpanzee beguiles itself by fiddling with the lock, and just happens to dial the combination by chance. The safe opens. The condition "Agent knows the combination of the safe" is clearly false, and so isn't a precondition. But nevertheless "Agent knows the combination of the safe" is a subgoal of the plan; all that has been demonstrated is that not all subgoals are preconditions of later actions.

This paper will claim that in order for a plan to be a good plan, the agent must "know how" to do all the actions in the plan, and that this need gives rise to knowledge subgoals just as preconditions of later actions give rise to world subgoals. All subgoals are to be satisfied by effects of earlier actions or the initial state.

There is also a quite different source of knowledge subgoals: the need to know which branch of any conditional to execute. In brief, if one accepts the formalism in this paper, such subgoals appear as conditions for the termination of plans. But I lack space to describe that here.

I will formalize what I think is going on in modal logic. Then the objects of belief and achievement can be represented as sentences. Lack of knowledge is an inability to distinguish states (or histories). This of course has been standard since Hintikka (1969) introduced epistemic logic. Not knowing what a term refers to amounts to it referring to different things in the various states that cannot be told apart.

Given that there are knowledge subgoals, there ought to be actions that can achieve them; and indeed there are. The effect of looking in a telephone directory under a given name is to know a telephone number; the effect of dipping litmus in a liquid is to know its acidity. That part of the puzzle of knowledge and action was well explained by Moore (1985), and this paper accepts his intuitions: essentially, knowledge-giving actions divide sets of indistinguishable states (or sequences of states, histories) into distinguishable sets. The liquid could be acid or alkaline; states differing on that point are indistinguishable; but once the litmus has been dipped in it, it turns blue or red, and states can no longer be confounded on that point.

Action descriptions, as well as object descriptions, may be uncertain. Since I do not know what "the combination of the safe" denotes, I cannot know which action "dialling the combination of the safe" corresponds to. In different states, it will denote different actions. The denotation of an action could be several things: I shall analyze it in two parts. There are things like jugs and tables and numbers and haircuts. These are things one can quantify over. Another sort of thing, rather more abstract, is action types. Action types map to state transitions, while jugs, numbers etc do not. Naturally each action type maps to the transition brought about by a performance of that type of action. Action types can exist at any convenient level of description.

At least for this paper, planning is finding terms that can be proved to denote action types with the right pre- and post-conditions. Since they are terms, they can be expressed to others.

What does "knowing how" to do A mean? There are two possible answers, corresponding to two ways that A could be a wanted part of the the plan. It could be there

i) because one wants to do the particular action A;

ii) because one wants a particular subgoal that A can achieve.

Here is an example of (i). John is playing a cello piece for his private enjoyment. At one point the score says "col legno". Now if John does not do exactly whatever playing col legno denotes, then he will not be playing the piece, and his intention will fail. John will believe that he knows how to play col legno only if he has no doubts about what action that term denotes - if it denotes the same action in all credible worlds. In this case John knows how to act because he has an EXACT description of what to do.

But if one wants to do A for reason (ii), to get its effect, "knowing how" may need less precision. Suppose that there are three half-inch spanners besides you, and John tells you to "pass him Tom's spanner". You can see that obviously John wants the spanner so that he can shift a half-inch nut. You may not not

know which spanner is Tom's. There are at least three credible worlds, differing
at least in which spanner Tom owns; and so in each of those three, the action
term "pass John Tom's spanner" denotes a different action. But for the purpose
of passing John a spanner, that does not matter. If you pass him any of them,
your purpose is achieved. For that purpose at any rate, you know how to act.
"Pass John Tom's spanner" is an ADEQUATE description of what you have to do.

Here is that distinction put more abstractly. There is a set of credible worlds.
There is an action term A. If A denotes the same action type at all credible
worlds, it is an exact description. Now suppose you have a goal S. If the action
denoted by A at any credible world W1 will, when performed in any credible world
W2, achieve S, then A is an adequate description.

I am interested in adequate descriptions.

Here is an example to show how getting information can make an action term
adequate, without anything else changing. Think again of John trying to open the
safe by dialling its combination. To make things simple, suppose the combination
is either 111 or 222. So "dial(combination(safe))" is at each world a term that
denotes an action that does, at that world, open the safe. But alas that
denotation is not constant - so the term is not exact. And more importantly its
denotation at some worlds (as it happens, at every world) is an action that will
fail to open the safe at some world. So it is not an adequate term either. That
can be drawn as figure A.

But suppose that John reads the manufacturer's slip which tells him what the
safe's combination is. Nothing else changes; but now the set of credible worlds
is divided so that in each part "dial(combination(safe))" denotes at every
credible world (as it happens, the only world) an action which at every credible
world (as it happens, the only world) opens the safe. The term is now adequate.
John now knows how to open the safe. That can be drawn as figure B.

Here is the intuition about the formalization. Space requires that I assume that
the reader knows epistemic and dynamic logics (Hintikka 1969) (Harel 1984). In
standard dynamic logic, an action modal such as "[A] S" talks about what
actually happens. I must add a construct that means "A is an adequate
description of an action to achieve S".

Suppose A is an atomic action. I seek to define << A >>, the relation on the set
of worlds that is denoted by the action term A when I am certain which world I
am in; and << uc A >>, when I act under uncertainty, because A has several
credible denotations. Assume that at each world i an action term A denotes a
relation on the set of worlds. Write that as m(A,i). For any relation R, define
x/R to be the set of things R-adjacent to x.

   x/R =def { y | <xy> ε R }

i) Certain execution

Now suppose I know exactly which world I am at (i, say). Then if I do the action
denoted by A, I will do m(A,i). That may vary from index to index. The
denotation of A is found by going to each index i, and collecting just the
transitions that leave i, according to the relation A denotes at i.

   << A >> = { <ij> | <ij> ε m(A,i) }

The situation is suggested in figure C.

ii) Uncertain execution

Now suppose I do not know exactly which world I am at. If I do the action denoted by A, I will do m(A,j), for some uncertain credible j. The denotation of A is found by going to each index i, and again collecting just the transitions that leave i, but now according to the relation that A denotes at any world credible at i.

$$<< uc\ A >>\ =\ \{\ <ik>\ |\ \exists j\ \varepsilon\ i/B.\ <ik>\ \varepsilon\ m(A,j)\ \}$$

The situation is suggested in figure D.

Observe that if I have complete accurate information about which world I am in - that is, if B is the diagonal relation on worlds, so $j\ \varepsilon\ i/B\ \equiv\ i=j$, then

$$<< uc\ A >>\ =\ << A >>$$

And if A denotes the same relation at all indices, so $m(A,i) = R(A)$ say, then

$$<< A >> = \{\ <ik>\ |\ <ik>\ \varepsilon\ R(A)\ \}\ =\ R(A)$$

which is the intuition of standard dynamic logic.

Now I identify the informal "A is an adequate description for achieving S" with

[uc A] S

when A is an atomic action or an atomic test.

It turns out to be impractical to define uncertain execution of complex actions, eg

uc (A;B)

Fortunately it is not necessary. What one needs is complex actions whose simple parts are executed under uncertainty.

(uc A) ; (uc B)

I shall now tidy up the proposal by presenting a logic of knowledge and action. I do not suggest reasoning in this logic. No-one would now propose to construct plans by theorem-proving in situation calculus. However, situation calculus is the logical justification of eg standard non-linear planning. I intend this logic to be the justification of sound, efficient, almost certainly incomplete planning programs.

The language is first-order, though names, functions, applications, and atomic sentences are presented via a typed language. This will pay off later when it comes to identifying expressions believed to have constant reference. The syntactic category of sentences "S" is a synonym for "Expr:t", the syntactic category of expressions denoting a truth value. All applications take one argument. The extension to zero or multiple arguments is trivial. There is no explicit abstraction. The typing is given by

           Type(e)   Type(t)   Type(a)

       if Type(X) then Type(e=>X)

A term such as "drop(vase)" will denote an object in the domain, an action type.
Which object it denotes may vary from index to index. Action types are a subset
of the domain. This means they can be quantified over, impossible in standard
DL. There is a syntactic category of "processes", expressions of the type
"...=>a". "drop" will be one of them. An object of type a such as the dropping
of a vase must be mapped to a relation on Indices; a function Do is provided to
do that.

It is important to be able to identify expressions (including action types) that
denote the same thing at all credible states. There is a construct to do that:

       ! Expr

The grammar exploits the fact that rewrite rules give sufficient, not precise,
conditions for membership of the category being defined in each rule. Missing
connectives come via the usual definitions.

       S ::=   S1 -> S2 | # | V Var:e. S | Bel S | ! Expr:X | [A] S
       Expr:X ::= Expr:Y=>X (Expr:Y) | Constant:X | Var:X
       Expr:e ::= Expr:a
       A ::= SimpleA | A1 ; A2 | A1 U A2 | A* | uc SimpleA
       SimpleA ::= Expr:a | S ?

An interpretation is a frame - a structure

       < Indices, B, Dom, ActionTypes, V, Do >

       Dom includes ActionTypes

TYPE interprets types in the usual way.

       TYPE(a) = ActionTypes   TYPE(e) = Dom   TYPE(t) = {0,1}
       TYPE(X=>Y) = TYPE(X)=>TYPE(Y)

There is a set of indices (states, worlds) Indices. B is a relation on Indices.
<ij> ε B iff j is compatible with what is believed at i. V interprets constants
in the usual way.

       V: Indices => Constant:X => TYPE(X)
       Do: ActionTypes => P(Indices X Indices)

         |= S iff V frames F. V i ε Indices of F. i |= S
       i |= S iff V g ε Var=>Dom. i g |= S

       i g |= S   abbreviates |[S]| i g = 1

       i g |= Expr:t if (not iff) |[Expr:t]| i g = 1
       i g |= S1 -> S2   iff i g |= S1   implies i g |= S2
       i g |= # is false
       i g |= V Var:e. S iff V d ε Dom. i g[Var:=d] |= S
       i g |= Bel S   iff V j ε i/B. j g |= S
       i g |= ! Expr:X iff ∃ x ε TYPE(X). V j ε i/B. |[Expr:X]| j g = x
       i g |= [A] S   iff V j (<ij> ε << A >> g). j g |= S

```
¦[ S ]¦ i g = if  i g ¦= S    then 1 else 0
¦[ Expr:X=>Y (Expr:X) ]¦ i g = (¦[ Expr:X=>Y ]¦ i g) (¦[ Expr:X ]¦ i g)
¦[ Constant:X ]¦ i g =  V i "Constant:X"
¦[ Var ]¦ i g =  g Var
```

<<.>> interprets programs or actions. (I shall not pass down g explicitly.)

```
<< A1 ; A2 >> = << A1 >> seq << A2 >>
<< A1 U A2 >> = << A1 >> U << A2 >>
<< A* >> = U n (0=<n, << A >>^n )

<< SimpleA >> =     ( <uv> ¦             <uv> ε (m "SimpleA" u) }

<< uc SimpleA >> =  ( <uv> ¦ ∃w ε u/B. <uv> ε (m "SimpleA" w) }
```

m: SimpleA => Indices => P(Indices x Indices)

```
m "Expr:a" i g =  Do( ¦[ Expr:a ]¦ i g)

m "S ?" i g =  ( <yy> ¦ i g ¦= S }
```

where seq is "left-to-right" composition, and if R is a relation on a set Set

```
R^0 = ( <ii> ¦ i ε Set } = diag Set      R^n+1 = R seq R^n
```

This semantics supports the axioms found in any "normal" modal logic. Here Modal is Bel or [A].

```
if ¦- S    then  ¦- Modal S
¦-  Modal (S -> T) -> Modal S -> Modal T
```

The standard dynamic logic axioms about complex actions are valid.

```
¦- [A] [B] S ≡ [A;B] S          ¦- [A] S & [B] S ≡ [AUB] S
¦- [A*] (S -> [A] S) -> (S -> [A*] S)
¦- [A*] S -> S                  ¦- [A*] S -> [A] [A*] S
¦- [ S? ] T ≡ (S -> T)
```

And so is this deceptively useless-looking axiom about uncertain tests.

```
¦- [ uc S? ] T  ≡  (-Bel -S) -> T
```

And so are these axioms about when terms denote the same thing at all credible states. This applies of course to names, but also to predicates and functions, and to sentences, which are expressions of type t.

```
¦- ! Expr1:X -> ! Expr2:X=>Y -> ! Expr1(Expr2)
¦- ! Var:X
¦- ! S  ≡ (K S v K -S)
```

There must also be axioms about when uncertain execution of a primitive action is adequate for a goal. The axioms listed so far, that follow just from the definition of a frame, are not enough. I have to make some assumptions about belief. This standard table relates properties of B and axioms about Bel.

```
B transitive           ¦- Bel S -> Bel Bel S
B euclidean            ¦- -Bel S -> Bel -Bel S
```

B serial |- Bel # -> #
B reflexive |- Bel S -> S

I assume that credible worlds may differ in what is true, but not in what one
believes. In that case

    j ε i/B -> i/B = j/B

It is easy to show that this condition is equivalent to requiring B to be both
transitive (I like my friends' friends) and euclidean (my friends like each
other). The other substantive assumption is that at least one state is credible,
so B is serial (I have a friend). Collectively, those imply

    |- Bel S ≡ Bel Bel S |- ! Expr ≡ Bel ! Expr

Notice that it is perfectly possible to be mistaken. That is, B may well not be
reflexive. So

    |/- Bel S -> S

Keep B transitive and euclidean. Suppose A denotes the same action at all
credible states, and that at all credible states certain execution of A achieves
S - that is, Bel [A] S is true. Then one must believe that which denotation of A
one executes and which state is actual is irrelevant - any pair will work. One
might expect

    |- ! A -> Bel([A] S ≡ [uc A] S)

And it is. And though I shall not discuss contingent plans in this paper, it is
useful that, if B is transitive and euclidean, the feeble-seeming

    |- [uc S?] T ≡ (-Bel -S) -> T

entails the much more useful

    |- [uc Bel S ?] Bel T ≡ Bel S -> Bel T

Here is the safe-opening example. The essence of plan construction is finding an
action description A, whose atomic actions are done under uncertainty, such that

    InitialState -> [A] Goals

I shall not present the complete proof, which is long and dull, but instead the
plan that is justified by the proof. It shows actions with their preconditions
and effects; ordering of actions; protected facts, guaranteed by some actions
and relied on by later ones; inferences, from some facts to others, drawn as
vertical lines. The only unusual part of this diagram is that each action A
gives rise automatically to the knowledge subgoal ! A, and protected facts drawn
above the actions are intended to guarantee those preconditions.

    Figure Plan

The proof is essentially applications of three sorts of inference:

i) Goal reduction like this

    |- Bel P -> [uc A] Bel Q |- Bel Q -> [uc B] Bel R

so   !- Bel P -> [uc A] [uc B] Bel R

so   !- Bel P - > [uc A ; uc B] Bel R

Axioms about domain actions have to be theorems, since they have to be true in
all states. In situation calculus that can be expressed by explicit universal
quantification over states. In STRIPS-type planners it is expressed as the
distinction between fixed and alterable axioms.

ii) Achieving constant designation of actions, so that uncertain execution is
adequate. That is by the axioms about ! Expr, and

        !- ! A -> Bel ([A] S ≡ [uc A] S)

iii) Use of frame axioms: axioms of the form

        !- S -> [A] S

The main moral of this is that it seems that ordinary non-linear planning will
generate plans with knowledge subgoals. All that is needed is automatic
generation of knowledge subgoals about constant designation of actions, which is
trivial. The fact that a technique is explained via modal logic does not mean
that its use requires full-blown modal logic theorem proving.

Conclusion

Knowledge subgoals (of one sort, anyhow) are systematically explicable. Once
explained, creating plans which recognize them and achieve them is much more
like ordinary domain planning that might be feared, and the changes needed to
ordinary planners look encouragingly slight.

Acknowledgements and related work

The intuition behind this paper was jointly discovered by Han Reichgelt and
myself. It was presented with a quite different formalization in (Steel
Reichgelt 1990).

A parallel approach to the work here is being pursued by Eric Werner at the
university of Hamburg (Werner 1989, 1990). He also uses modal logic to represent
the interaction of knowledge and ability, but does it using notions of strategy
drawn from decision theory. I view his work as complementary, not alternative.

Despite disagreeing with it, I wish to draw attention to related work reported
in (Davis Morgenstern Sanders (eds) 1989) and (Morgenstern 1989).

References

Davis E; Morgenstern L; Sanders K (eds):1989. IJCAI workshop on knowledge,
perception and planning. (Detroit: 1989)
Harel, D: 1984. Dynamic logic. chap II.10, 497-604 of: Gabbay, Dov; Guenthner, F
(eds): 1984. Handbook of philosophical logic. D. Reidel
Hintikka, J: 1962. Knowledge and belief. Cornell UP: Ithaca, NY
Moore, Robert: 1985. A formal theory of knowledge and action. in: Hobbs JR,
Moore RC: 1985. Formal theories of the commonsense world. Norwood, NJ: Ablex
publishing corp.
Morgenstern, Leora: 1987. Knowledge preconditions for actions and plans. IJCAI-
87 867-874
Steel SWD, Reichgelt H. 1990. Knowing how and finding out. Proc. ninth

meeting UK special interest group on planning. Nottingham: April 1990
Werner, Eric: 1989. Modal Logic of Games. WISBER Report Nr. B48, University of
Saarbruecken
Werner, Eric: 1990. A unified view of information, intention and ability. Second
European Workshop on modelizing autonomous agents and multi-agent worlds. (St
Quentin en Yvelines; Aug 1990; ONERA) 69-83

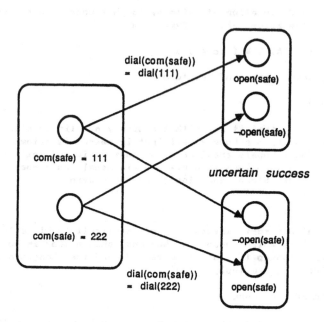

Figure A

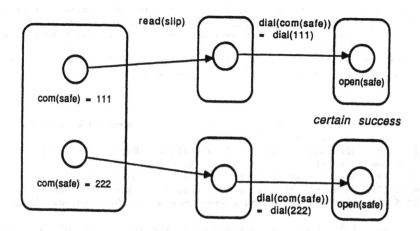

Figure B

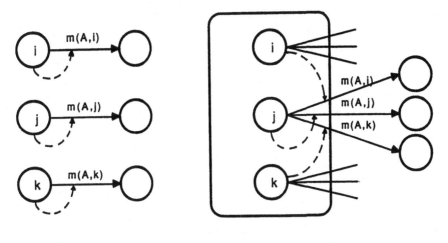

Figure C   Figure D

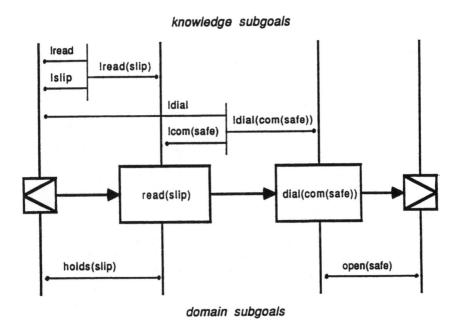

knowledge subgoals

domain subgoals

Figure plan

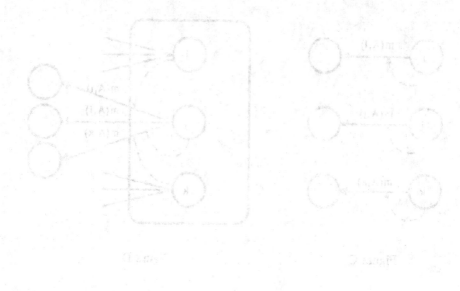

Lecture Notes in Artificial Intelligence (LNAI)

Lecture Notes in Computer Science